Discovering the Benefits of Effective Portfolios

Discovering the Benefits of Effective Portfolios

Innovative Solutions for the Implementation of Grading Academic Work

M. Scott Norton

ROWMAN & LITTLEFIELD
Lanham • Boulder • New York • London

Published by Rowman & Littlefield
An imprint of The Rowman & Littlefield Publishing Group, Inc.
4501 Forbes Boulevard, Suite 200, Lanham, Maryland 20706
www.rowman.com

6 Tinworth Street, London SE11 5AL, United Kingdom

Copyright © 2021 by M. Scott Norton

All rights reserved. No part of this book may be reproduced in any form or by any electronic or mechanical means, including information storage and retrieval systems, without written permission from the publisher, except by a reviewer who may quote passages in a review.

British Library Cataloguing in Publication Information Available

Library of Congress Cataloging-in-Publication Data

Names: Norton, M. Scott, author.
Title: Discovering the benefits of effective portfolios : innovative solutions for the implementation of grading academic work / M. Scott Norton.
Description: Lanham : Rowman & Littlefield, [2021] | Includes bibliographical references. | Summary: "The book is intended to serve as a valuable resource/strategy for assessing and evaluating learning during the pandemic but will continue to be of primary help to students and teachers after the pandemic reaches its end"— Provided by publisher.
Identifiers: LCCN 2021009863 (print) | LCCN 2021009864 (ebook) | ISBN 9781475860450 (cloth) | ISBN 9781475860467 (paperback) | ISBN 9781475860474 (epub)
Subjects: LCSH: Portfolios in education—United States. | Grading and marking (Students)—United States.
Classification: LCC LB1029.P67 N67 2021 (print) | LCC LB1029.P67 (ebook) | DDC 371.27/20973—dc23
LC record available at https://lccn.loc.gov/2021009863
LC ebook record available at https://lccn.loc.gov/2021009864

Contents

Preface: Why This Book Was Written ... ix
How This Book Is Organized ... x

1 Assessing and Evaluating a Student's Educational Progress: The Student Portfolio as an Answer to Student Grading ... 1
Special Problems of Grading during the Covid-19 Pandemic ... 2
Student Grading as a Meaningful Process ... 2
Student Grading: The Way Things Are Done around Here ... 3
The Search for a Better Answer ... 3
Just What Is a Portfolio? ... 4
The Student Learning Portfolio: A Purposeful Way to Assess Students' Learning ... 6
The Working Portfolio: The Heart of the Program ... 6
The Enhancement of Research Methodology ... 8
The Research on Portfolios ... 8
The Opportunities for Students to Initiate Research Methods ... 8
Student Progress and the Showing of a Student's Best Work ... 9
Beginning with a Focus on Purpose ... 10
The Student Portfolio and How It Promotes Effective Learning ... 10
Student Portfolios Assume a Variety of Educational Purposes ... 12
Special Benefits of a Student Portfolio ... 12
What Content Commonly Is Included in a Student Portfolio? ... 13
How Do School Personnel View Portfolio Learning? ... 14

	A Lightbulb Experience!	15
	Student Portfolio Assessment and Evaluation	16
	Student Portfolios and Their Benefits for School Administration	17
	The Implementation of Student Portfolios in Practice	17
	Attempts to Determine the Extent of Portfolio Utilization Today	18
	Portfolios and Their Planning and Implementation: A Collaborative Program	20
	Student Portfolios Do Have Problems amid Controversial Issues	20
	What Is the Status of Student Portfolios in School Programs Nationally?	22
	Key Chapter Ideas and Recommendations	24
	References	25
2	The World of Portfolios: How Portfolios Are Used, Assessed, and Evaluated	27
	More Examples of Learning Portfolios and How They Are Assessed and Evaluated	27
	A Rubric Scoring Guide for One Type of a Portfolio	28
	Examples of Other Rubrics for Scoring Student Portfolios	29
	Summary of How Student Portfolios Can Be Most Helpful When Used in the Classroom, Wherever That Might Be	29
	The Nominal Group Technique	30
	The *Delphi Technique*	30
	In Troubled Times, Communication Tends to Become Problematic	31
	Best Works Portfolios: Showing the Highest Level of a Student's Achievement	32
	Assessment Portfolios: Demonstrating the Student's Mastery of Learnings	33
	Portfolio Assessment at the Elementary School Level	34
	A Review Quiz for Chapters 1 and 2	35
	Answers to the Quiz	37
	Your Quiz Score	38
	A Chapter Summary Statement	39
	Key Chapter Ideas and Recommendations	40
	References	41

3	Portfolios with Many Purposes	43
	Portfolio Development and Evaluation Procedures for Educational Administration Including Curriculum and Supervision	44
	An Example of a Student Portfolio	44
	Portfolio Assessment and Evaluation	46
	Cases of Unsatisfactory Portfolios	47
	A Scoring Rubric for a Completed Portfolio	48
	Examples of Scoring Rubrics for Student Portfolios	48
	Student Portfolios, Yes, But What about Teaching Portfolios?	49
	The Contents of a Teaching Portfolio	51
	Professional Growth and Development	53
	The Lightbulb Blew Out	54
	A Closer Look at Student Learning Styles: A Must for Effective Teaching	56
	Key Chapter Ideas and Recommendations	57
	References	58
4	Important Portfolios with Various Purposes	59
	Portfolios for Educational Administrator Program Admission, Programs of Study, and Field Experiences	60
	Leaders' Program Portfolios	60
	The Learning Benefits of Student Portfolios as Stated by Faculty Personnel	64
	An Interesting Side Note: Portfolios Completed Online	64
	A Supplemental Discussion of Teaching Portfolios: Similarities of K–12 and Higher Education Portfolio Products	66
	Portfolios Utilized in University/College Preparation Programs	68
	Portfolio Clarifications	69
	Presentation of the Student Portfolio	70
	The Contents and Makeup of the Student Portfolio	71
	Presenting the Portfolio	72
	Portfolio Assessment and Evaluation	73
	Portfolio Projects for Courses in Higher Education	74
	Critical Thinking through Reflection: Artifacts	74
	A Change of Place: The Wide Utilization of Business Portfolios	76
	A Four-Chapter True/False Quiz	80

Answers to the Quiz 81
Your Quiz Score 84
Key Chapter Ideas and Recommendations 84
References 85

About the Author 87

Preface
Why This Book Was Written

The assessment and grading of students' work in grades K–12 and higher education have been somewhat problematic historically. The subjectiveness of the assessment and evaluation by teachers all too often has influenced grades of A through F. That is, not only have test results been used as the basis for letter grades, but such things as student behavior, absenteeism, personality characteristics, and the philosophy of the school have entered the assessment and evaluation results.

In addition, any attempts to change grading systems commonly have been met with parent criticism since *understanding* of a new procedure has been difficult for parents. The historical grades of A or F are readily recognized by all those concerned. A grade of *A* means tops and a grade of *F* means failure.

In any case, just what learning did take place is not defined by letter grades. Just what the student knows about the subject is not projected in the letter grade system. A better assessment and grading practices are needed. Some strategy is needed to provide an ongoing opportunity for the student and teacher to assess and evaluate the student's actual growth that has taken place over a specified period of time.

Various leaders in education have supported the concept of student portfolios for academic assessment and evaluation. One widely accepted answer to meet this need is the student portfolio which is discussed in depth throughout this book. However, portfolios have proven of great benefit not only in education programs but in business and industrial practices as well. The many benefits of administration/management portfolios are given major attention through the chapters of this book.

The ongoing Covid-19 pandemic that was occurring during the writing of this book has promoted the implementation of student and teaching portfolios nationally. It seems clear that the closing of many schools and the attempt to implement virtual learning that takes place primarily in the home would be a beneficial answer to the student grading question. The contents of a portfolio and the rubrics used to assess and evaluate the end product center on what was actually learned by the student as well as the quality of the learning.

It must be underlined that the book's content goes far beyond that of student portfolios. A wide variety of portfolios for teachers, administrators, businesses, and industries is included in the chapter discussions. The key word, perhaps, for an effective portfolio is that of *purpose*. A portfolio serves several important purposes that include meaningful grading but also a way to keep the learner directly involved in the learning process.

What the student actually has learned along with his or her strengths and weaknesses come to the fore. The student's main interests and needs are brought to the attention of the teachers and parents. In short, the student's specific interests and needs are brought to the learner's attention. The results of the student's work give the learner an important role in his/her learning process as well as providing an answer to the effectiveness of the choices he or she has made to reach the level of learning realized at a specific point and time.

HOW THIS BOOK IS ORGANIZED

The title of the book, *Discovering the Benefits of Effective Portfolios*, expresses the fact that various types of portfolios can serve students, teachers, administrators, and workers in the areas of business and industry in positive/beneficial ways. The processes for student learning during the recent Covid-19 pandemic have been troublesome at best. Schools have closed, reopened, and then closed once again. The effectiveness of homeschooling and virtual learning is yet to be determined. The book is intended to serve as a valuable resource/strategy for assessing and evaluating learning during the pandemic but will continue to be of primary help to students and teachers after the pandemic reaches its end.

The book's contents include four chapters centering on an in-depth discussion of the purposes of portfolios and their wide uses in education, business, and other management areas. Chapter 1 explains the various contents of portfolios and their underlying purposes. The ways in which student portfolios can enrich the growth and development of the student are presented, and the special procedures for portfolio "grading" are set forth in detail in chapter 2. Grading by the use of rubrics serves several major learning outcomes as well as how the student becomes a primary participant in his or her learning program.

Chapter 3 focuses on many examples of portfolios that are utilized in K–12 schools to assess and evaluate student growth and development. Other portfolios, such as teacher portfolios, are introduced as well. Scoring of portfolios, which eliminates the common grading methods used in schools today, are presented along with examples of the use of scoring rubrics that demonstrate the effectiveness of the students' learning growth. Teacher portfolios are viewed as being of paramount importance for helping the teachers be most effective in his or her growth and development program activities. Chapter 4 introduces the benefits of portfolios in business management and other administrative programs. The most common contents of business portfolios are set forth along with the rubrics utilized for assessing and evaluating their effectiveness.

A four-chapter quiz is set forth that will be of benefit for students, teachers, administrators, and others for re-examining their gains in portfolio knowledge and skills. Chapter 4 includes a final summary in the way of "Key Chapter Ideas and Recommendations." Each chapter of the book contains such a summary for the primary purpose of underscoring the most important aspects of the chapter.

As intended, the book serves a vital purpose of presenting an important answer to the present grading problems faced by schools across the nation. Portfolios not only serve as a more effective assessment and evaluation strategy than the common letter grade procedure utilized in school program, but enhances the understanding of students, parents, teachers, and administrators as to what has actually been learned and what additional learning needs must be addressed.

Chapter 1

Assessing and Evaluating a Student's Educational Progress

The Student Portfolio as an Answer to Student Grading

Primary chapter goal—To set forth a comprehensive concept relative to the purpose and benefits of a student learning portfolio and others for assessing and evaluating the educational development of individual students and how it could serve as a beneficial learning document during troubled times such as the virus pandemic. In addition, problems related to the implementation of portfolios in practice are considered.

The assessment and grading of students in grades K–12 have been confronted with various problems of accuracy, fairness, objectivity, and value. Basing a student's grade on 'what was learned' commonly is undermined by the subjectivity of student behavior, student/teacher relationships, and other affective traits that influence the teacher's judgment of the actual learning outcomes. Just what to include in judging the grade of any one student becomes problematic.

Should grades be based solely on final test results? What about grading homework or student contributions to class discussions and other activities? No single criterion is sufficient to provide what was learned by the student in the present class at hand. Since different teachers commonly use different information for grading purposes, just what learning has taken place when a grade of 'A' is awarded is not clear. The student has met the teacher's expectations for the course but the extent of the student's gained knowledge and skill has not been demonstrated effectively.

SPECIAL PROBLEMS OF GRADING DURING THE COVID-19 PANDEMIC

The problems of grading the learning of students through homeschooling or other digital learning devices are troublesome. Teachers tend to conjure up various grading procedures such as pass/fail results, credits earned, grade promotion on condition, or other nebulous labels that gave little evidence as to what was learned or not learned in the course or grade at hand. There is a great need to find an alternative for the common classroom testing procedures. Some strategy is needed whereby the learning of the student is demonstrated by the growth made over a specific period of time. Additionally, the strategy should be instrumental in providing the student with evidence of his or her strengths and the growth that has taken place during the learning period.

STUDENT GRADING AS A MEANINGFUL PROCESS

Historically, educators have emphasized the principle that the needs and interests of the student are of paramount importance for an effective learning process. Yet, school programs seldom take such a principle seriously. Curricula, activities, procedures, and 'assessments' of the student's learning are primarily boiler plated by the school and the school teacher. Student involvement in the process is missing since the learning program is decided primarily by required courses and a few electives. As a result, students have little or no understanding of what goes into the process of grading. What a grade of 'A' means in a course in history is likely to be viewed quite differently in a course in mathematics. What did I learn to receive a grade of 'A' is a question for the most part that remains unanswered.

An effective learning strategy should provide an ongoing opportunity for the student and teacher(s) to assess and evaluate the student's learning growth. Both the strengths and weaknesses of the student's learning choices should be evaluated and assessed. It is common to hear the statement that education of a student should take into consideration his or her interests and needs. This involvement statement suggests, first and foremost, that learning should be carried out with the important involvement of the learner. Learning purposes, choices, and results must be of primary interest to the student. Student motivation looms important.

STUDENT GRADING: THE WAY THINGS ARE DONE AROUND HERE

The responsibility for teachers to give students specific grades for their performance in an academic area or program activity has been a problem in classrooms across the nation. There are approximately 3.2 million public school teachers assigning scholastic grades to students using what they view as fair and objective grading methods. Yet, a close examination of teachers' grading methods reveal great differences in how academic subjects are graded, whether number grades, letter grades, pass-fail grades, or some other grading system are utilized. How much student thought is given to what learning activities that students undertake? This is a question that needs to be answered.

Without question, student grading is one of the *bugaboos* that face teachers in the elementary and secondary grade levels. With more than a million public school teachers having the responsibility for student grades in their classrooms, it takes little imagination to know that teacher grading opens the door widely for subjectivity relative to what a student actually has learned.

One teacher reported that she eliminated (almost) all grading problems in her classroom. It was not clear what the school or school district grading system policy required, but this teacher made a ruling of no Fs or zeroes. It is either A, B, C, or 'incomplete.' This is one teacher's rationale for a grading procedure, but having over 1 million teachers nationally come up with their own ideas of what is best does little to resolve the grading dilemmas that face the nation's schools.

THE SEARCH FOR A BETTER ANSWER

The traditional methods of grading students with letter or number grades (i.e., As to Fs or 1s to 5s) are virtually impossible to change. It's the only methods that have been in place for decades and the only ones that parents appear to accept. Few parents could explain the nature of a student portfolio. In addition, programs in higher education only want to know about the student's GPA score and results on one or two standardized tests. Grading scores represented by the terms *exemplary, proficient, emerging,* and *unacceptable* are foreign in the minds of most persons. Grades of As to Fs or 1s to

5s historically have been used in elementary and secondary schools as well as in most institutions of higher learning.

To what extent do letter and number grades indicate what the student has learned in the courses/activities at hand? It is common for students in academic subjects to receive a final grade based on the course's final test. The final test might indicate what the student knows about what was on the final test, but what actually has been learned in the course remains incomplete. The final test would indicate only what the student knew about the problems in that test. Many of the arithmetical concepts actually learned in grade 3, but not tested, are likely to be of most importance for progressing successfully in grade 4. Thus, the final test merely indicates what the student knows about the questions on that specific test.

Many other judgment factors enter into most grading systems. The student's attitude toward learning, classroom behavior, completion of homework, attention/participation in class activities, absenteeism, the positiveness of teacher and student relationships, the grading philosophy of the school district, and other judgmental characteristics tend to influence the grades of the student. Just what has been learned can easily be overlooked. What is needed is a strategy that provides an ongoing opportunity for the student and teacher to assess and evaluate the student's learning growth including strengths and weaknesses and the effectiveness of the learning choices that the student and teacher have employed. When properly done, student portfolios can serve to motivate the students to assume more responsibility for what and how they learn.

JUST WHAT IS A PORTFOLIO?

Norton (2004) defined *a portfolio* as an organized, goal-driven documentation of one's professional growth and achievement experiences. Each word in the definition expresses the substance of an effective portfolio. First, an effective student portfolio is planned and organized. It is a purposeful document underscored by goals and objectives. It is personal in its makeup in revealing one's overall development. It demonstrates the student's personal and professional growth and achievements.

The term *portfolio* stems from the Latin roots of *porta*, meaning to carry, and *folio*, meaning page or sheet. In its best form, the portfolio sets forth a great deal of information about who you are, what you have done, what you plan to do, and where you hope to go. The contents set forth in a personal portfolio contain the evidence that you are or perhaps you are not prepared to do what the portfolio purposes had established for you. The concept of portfolios and their presence in contemporary practice might be somewhat surprising to the reader. Their implementation for student learning during troublesome times, such as the virus pandemic, most likely will bring portfolios to the front of educational practices in K–12 schools and student courses in higher education as well.

Certainly, portfolios are not new to the profession of education or to other professions such as architecture, business, law, engineering, art, and sales. In the profession of education, portfolios historically have been used for such purposes as internship logs, field project journals, activity mapping, specific course learnings, and as a means to reveal personal growth and development. Since there are so many different purposes of portfolios in education (e.g., learning, advising, employment, designing, assessment, and evaluation), some authorities have expressed the opinion that every portfolio should have a modifier or adjective that describes its purpose (Barrett 2020, August 27).

In addition, Barrett notes that research shows that students at all levels see assessment that is done by someone else to show them what they thought of it. Besides just seeing a grade of B or a few grammatical corrections, the student learns little about what was learned or what was actually considered in deciding the grade given the product. What criteria were put into play that determined a grade of A, B, or C? Barrett argues that students benefit from an awareness of the processes and strategies involved in writing, solving a problem, researching a topic, analyzing information, or having an opportunity to learn why a grade of A or D was given a class product. Quality student portfolios have high potential for meeting a student's interests and needs.

Evans set forth a rather unique definition of a portfolio by defining a portfolio

> as an ongoing collection of personal thoughts about one's goals and experiences that is accompanied by reflection and self-assessments . . . It represents who you are, what you are, where you have been, where you are, where you want to go, and how you plan on getting there. (Evans 1995, p. 11)

THE STUDENT LEARNING PORTFOLIO: A PURPOSEFUL WAY TO ASSESS STUDENTS' LEARNING

Danielson and Abrutyn (1997) authored a book on the topic of how student portfolio purpose is illustrated. Note that the book was published 24 years ago. These authors identified working portfolios, display, showcase, or best works portfolios, assessment portfolios, subject area portfolios, and skill area portfolios. Although the titles of the various kinds of portfolios have tended to change over the years, the content and purposes of the portfolios tend to be similar. When it comes to student portfolios, purpose becomes the guiding light. It is of some importance to point out that there are many different types/kinds of portfolios in education, business, and other professions.

THE WORKING PORTFOLIO: THE HEART OF THE PROGRAM

The *working portfolio* is especially designed to be used to evaluate whether the actual learning activities are performed in the school classroom, completed digitally, or presented using various homeschooling strategies. A *best works portfolio* displays a student's best or high-quality contents and results in providing a sense of accomplishment on the part of the student.

Danielson and Abrutyn (1997) viewed the working portfolio as a project in the works that ultimately is placed in the work folder. In any case, a working portfolio serves to hold information for possible work to be utilized later for more permanent assessment and evaluation. Once again, a working portfolio is based on important learning objectives/purposes related to the interests and needs of the individual learner. In this sense, the working portfolio gives the student/teacher evidence of the student's strengths and weakness and thus is beneficial for determining the future curricular program objectives for the learner.

In an effort to find better ways of assessing student progress, some high schools have implemented student portfolios. Not only have the student portfolios provided improved information relative to the presence of student learning, but those educators using portfolios have underscored their value for increasing the potential of success in higher education programs. Final course examinations have tended to be utilized in many schools for determining a student's final course grade. A student portfolio in most cases represents the work/learning of a student over a long period of time. Portfolio users have strong beliefs that such strategies give important support for collaborative learning, critical thinking, and for ongoing opportunities for the student to be directly involved in his or her personal learning program.

We frequently hear the phrase that leaning should be closely tied to each individual's interests and needs. When the student has the ongoing opportunity to help determine his or her learning plan, the principle of 'interest and needs' becomes more of a reality. Some authorities refer to the student completed portfolio as 'performance-based assessments.' Ongoing opportunities to assess and evaluate learning results support the important purposes for the learning to keep researching, keep learning, and keep finding the best answers to problems and questions posed. In the long run, what actually is included in the student's portfolio is indeed his or her best work.

Hopkinson (2017) points out an additional plus related to student portfolio strategies. It is common for students to be required to stand before his or her peers and present their work on the portfolio. This procedure is quite different that just receiving a test score whereby only the student and the teachers know the end product and the grade for its accomplishment. Such collaborative experiences tend to benefit the individual learner as well as the students who are collaborating in group sessions. Once again, the important learning factor of collaboration comes into play. Learning from one another is not only welcomed, it is promoted.

The implementation of portfolios in education is inhibited in many instances due to the fact that the purposes of their implementation have not been adequately disseminated. Changing from a letter grade or a number grade to a new assessment strategy does not come easily. Since the implementation of student portfolios can serve a variety of purposes, the use of the student portfolio must be made clear to all those concerned. The questions as to how the portfolio is to be utilized, the expected term of the portfolio, the specific skills and knowledge to be viewed as center stage, the extent that the student's parents are to be involved in the planning and execution of the portfolio plan, whether the portfolio plan is to be passed on to others for instructional purposes, and just how the portfolio is to be assessed, evaluated, and graded must be attended as well. The processes of assessment and evaluation of student portfolios are discussed in-depth in a later chapter of the book.

THE ENHANCEMENT OF RESEARCH METHODOLOGY

Although the working portfolio is most helpful to the student and the teacher, parents have found it to be of great benefit in informing them about the efficacy of the school's education program and the effectiveness of its instructional procedures. Rather than letting a grade of 'C' determine the actual progress of a student's English communication, the working portfolio contains actual evidence of the student's written communication and can include recorded speech evidence set forth by the student as well.

A periodic assessment and evaluation of the student's portfolio provides specific evidence of the student's learning progress in relation to the purposes/standards that were established at the outset of the portfolio planning. What goals and objectives have been accomplished and how are these accomplishments evidenced in the contents of the portfolio? As a student progresses on a working portfolio, various information and examples of work can be moved to other more specific purposes as related to the student's future educational program/instruction.

THE RESEARCH ON PORTFOLIOS

The following sections center on the kinds and extent of research that has focused on portfolio utilization in education and in other businesses. Although specific research studies on portfolio utilization will be presented, the following general information establishes the common uses of portfolios in administrative preparation programs. In following sections of this chapter, examples of various portfolio research are presented.

As noted in table 1.1, the primary uses of education portfolios centered on academic/program activities as opposed to such requirements as program admission and continuation.

THE OPPORTUNITIES FOR STUDENTS TO INITIATE RESEARCH METHODS

A primary benefit of student portfolio development is that of introducing the concepts of empirical and basic research. In one sense, the implementation

Table 1.1 Portfolio Uses in Preparation Programs

	% Response
a. Requirement for an internship	73.7
b. Part of course requirements	52.6
c. In lieu of a comprehensive exam	47.4
d. Evaluation of administrative skills at the beginning, middle, or end of program	42.1
e. Fieldwork or other practicum	36.8
f. Entry year assessment requirement	10.6
g. Decide continuation in program	10.6
h. Part of state's requirements	10.6
i. Exploration of research/dissertation topic	5.3
j. Admission requirement	5.3

of research methods in portfolio development carries with it the important characteristic of 'critical thinking' and problem-solving. Give thought to the common procedure for a research project that includes: a statement of the problem/question to be answered, the necessary review of the literature, the procedures for the collection of related data for the application/treatment of the data relative to the question/hypothesis at hand, and the decision-making process that leads to answering the question(s) posed.

STUDENT PROGRESS AND THE SHOWING OF A STUDENT'S BEST WORK

As previously noted, a student learning portfolio serves several important purposes. It is an effective way to assess students' learning while keeping them directly involved in the learning process. The factors relating to how the student has grown over a specified period of time and the effectiveness of the learning choices can be determined. Academic strengths of the student come to the fore and the areas of 'additional learning' are brought to the learner's attention. Such personal assessments give the learner an important role in the learning process as well as providing evidence relative to the effectiveness of the choices that he or she has made to reach the level of learning realized at some point and time. The goal of getting the student involved in his or her personal learning can be facilitated by an effective implementation of the portfolio process.

BEGINNING WITH A FOCUS ON PURPOSE

The title of this chapter, "Assessing and Evaluating a Student's Educational Progress: The Student Portfolio as an Answer to Student Grading," suggests that student portfolios can serve as important grading tools during normal and troubled times. During the troubled times of the Covid-19 pandemic, problems related to the opening of schools and the ways and means for determining the growth of students, who are working primarily at home, have not been determined successfully to date.

The nature of student learning portfolios and their intended purposes are discussed in-depth in the following sections of chapter 1. Purpose serves as the leading focus of the following discussions. Purpose promotes student interest which facilitates motivation and learning accomplishments.

THE STUDENT PORTFOLIO AND HOW IT PROMOTES EFFECTIVE LEARNING

Most commonly, a student portfolio is a collection of the academic work of a student accompanied by various examples that show the quality level of the student's work, the progress that the student has made during a specific time period, the extent to which the student has dealt with the required standards set forth in relation to the course or activity at hand, and the extent to which the information serves to strengthen the achievement of the student's goals and objectives. This means that a quality student portfolio must include several quality characteristics:

- A *quality portfolio* must be clearly defined by purpose, procedures, and supervisory/teacher roles and responsibilities. There are various kinds of student portfolios, and the purpose of each kind must be fully understood. This characteristic includes knowing the standards and requirements that are related to the major purpose of the portfolio in hand. Local, state, and federal requirements/standards must be defined and expertly understood. These program requirements reveal the important need for student involvement in their own learning.
- Understanding of the specific requirements/standards related to the initiation, adoption, and implementation of the portfolio and its processes

is essential. In brief, details of how the portfolio is to be initiated and when it is scheduled to become operational are of paramount importance. Who is to be the teacher and/or supervisor regarding the implementation of the portfolio, its assessment, and evaluation sessions? What are the required completion requirements that the student must meet? Such questions must be understood at the outset of the portfolio's initiation.

The listing of the portfolio's contents must be determined at the outset of its initiation. However, assessment and evaluation sessions, that take place during the completion of the portfolio, hold implications for the portfolio's requirements. Thus, additions and changes in the portfolio's contents are appropriate and needed in the best interests of the student's learning program. The student will benefit a great deal by giving serious thought and discussion to the contents of the portfolio. Commonly, the contents of the student portfolio include the following information:

- The recording of the portfolio content and experiences
- Documentation of special activities (i.e., field experiences, research results, and publications/presentations)
- Courses taken and results
- Internships/presentations
- Workshops/conferences
- Testing requirements, tests completed, and testing results
- Other appropriate information that serves to demonstrate new growth and development
- Projections for completion of the portfolio
- Specific directions for the assessment and evaluation of the portfolio (i.e., evaluation by student and teacher/supervisor, faculty input as fits the case, oral defense if portfolio is part of a graduation program or certification program.)
- Specific requirements stating what is required in the unfortunate case that the portfolio completion is not approved as being unsatisfactory.

Nevertheless, a faculty evaluation procedure should be withheld by the teacher/supervisor and serve to set forth follow-up procedures that the student must complete satisfactorily.

STUDENT PORTFOLIOS ASSUME A VARIETY OF EDUCATIONAL PURPOSES

The initiation and completion of a student portfolio should be governed by the three Ps: Purpose, Purpose and Purpose. The reader should understand that there are many different kinds of portfolios. The most common purposes/benefits of a student portfolio include: (1) evaluating course work quality, learning progress, and academic achievement; such evaluation must be done on a regular basis rather than just at the end of a required course or the school year; (2) determining whether students have met *learning standards* or other academic requirements for courses, grade-level promotion, and graduation; helping students reflect on their academic goals and progress as learners; thus such assessments/evaluation must be regular and ongoing and not just at the end of a course or school year; and (3) creating a lasting archive of academic work products, accomplishments, and other documentation of knowledge and skills on the part of the learner.

Thus, portfolios cannot only be used to reveal what has been learned but also come into active play to test whether the student can apply the learning to issues and/or problems faced in various fields such as economics, history, and business practices.

Authorities 'argue' that student portfolios serve to provide a richer, deeper, and more accurate picture of what students have learned and are able to do more than traditional measures such as standardized tests, quizzes, or final exams that only measure what students know at a specific point in time. We commend the foregoing definition by the Glossary of Education reform. We discuss the perspectives set forth by the foregoing definition of a portfolio in this chapter and also in each of the following chapters of the book.

SPECIAL BENEFITS OF A STUDENT PORTFOLIO

Student portfolios do have common characteristics and are utilized for a large number of educational purposes. Most commonly, a student portfolio is a collection of the academic learnings and other educational information that serves to assess and evaluate work completed for a specific course. Whether or not the student has learned the information requirements of the course is a question of primary importance. In addition, such a portfolio helps the student toward self-evaluation strategies that serve to help the student understand whether or not he or she has met the required learning standards for passing the course, moving to the next grade level, being promoted, or graduating from one educational level to the next higher level.

A student portfolio can be especially beneficial in helping the student assess their personal progress toward meeting a specific academic goal. Self-evaluation opportunities are ongoing when portfolio procedures are being carried out effectively. Although there is a large variety of student portfolios designed by teachers for their course purposes, most commonly there are three types of student portfolios. Some portfolios include specific examples of a student's work accomplished in respect to what he or she is required to know. Certain cognitive skills, such as specific knowledge, needed preparation for a field of work, principles of organization, effective teaching strategies, communication skills, and others, serve as the focus of this type of portfolio. Such portfolios are termed *assessment portfolios*.

Working portfolios, on the other hand, commonly center on whether the student is currently working and what learning is taking place that enhances his or her knowledge and competency for the required work. In this case, the individual will describe and/or provide specific examples of the current working activities. Special achievements and basic knowledge requirements, commonly required for the job, are described in the individual's portfolio by way of work experience, work time allotments, and significant work accomplishments.

Display portfolios are ones in which students, teachers, administrators, and others set forth displays of their most impressive work accomplishments by summarizing special knowledge, giving examples of work accomplishments, showing evidence of one's best work, and presenting any awards, recognitions, or innovative recommendations that a company or industry might utilize. In any case, the display portfolio reveals the best work of a student or other individual such as a teacher or school administrator.

WHAT CONTENT COMMONLY IS INCLUDED IN A STUDENT PORTFOLIO?

Melissa Kelly (2019, November 14) suggests that there are certain contents that should be included in a student portfolio. Although Kelly notes that items to include vary by grade and subject, the important thing to remember is that the portfolio should paint a detailed and accurate picture of a student's skills and abilities. She lists 16 specific items to be included. Five of the 16 items should be sufficient to demonstrate the complexity of the student portfolio: (1) a letter to the reader outlining each portfolio item; (2) a collection of goals for the year, selected and updated by students monthly; (3) sample essays of writing featuring a few key writing techniques; (4) creative writing samples; and (5) reading logs.

Yes, quality student portfolios take considerable time, but so does sitting in a classroom for a full semester. Portfolio requirements reveal the important need for the student and teacher to work cooperatively at the outset to give serious attention to the purposes, contents, time factors, and related work requirements that must be attended during the completion of the portfolio. The residual benefits of the student portfolio become evident as well. Helping students prepare for college, intensified teacher/student collaboration, the focus on the student's best work, critical thinking requirements, performance-based learning, learning evidence in hand, potential for student collaboration/support, emphasis on organization, research skills, accountability measures, and other cognitive and affective characteristics are needed in completion of a quality student portfolio.

HOW DO SCHOOL PERSONNEL VIEW PORTFOLIO LEARNING?

High schools in California have formed networks to promote performance-based assessment strategies, including student portfolios. In one survey, school principals valued the contents of a portfolio as being beneficial with 83.3% of them agreeing that they provide evidence of organization and planning skills. Other leaders have underscored the value of portfolios as facilitating student/teacher collaboration, fostering preliminary research skills, and providing 'official' opportunities for student speaking experience. For example, collaboration looms important during the completion of the portfolio and during the required 'defense' of the portfolio before a faculty group or other evaluation/assessment group within the school community.

Reports indicate that student portfolios are becoming more popular generally and more specifically in more areas of the school curriculum. Collaboration in learning has risen in popularity in the last few years. Rather than stressing the importance of doing your own work, open classrooms have been instrumental in purposely promoting groups of students to study and learn together. Best solutions and extended knowledge tend to accompany group learning sessions. Cooperative learning groups serve to give learners a chance to listen to another student's ideas relative to their work. The best idea might well be exposed through a positive cooperative action of a learning group.

A LIGHTBULB EXPERIENCE!

One group of grade 7 learners were developing a piece for their student portfolios on number systems. Each participant had explained in some depth the concept of the common number system based on the number 10. That is, the number 37 is represented by 7 units and 3 tens. The number 1,269 is 9 units + 6 tens + 2 hundreds + 1 thousands (9 + 60 + 200 + 1,000). The common number system is based on the decimal system of 10: units, tens, hundreds, thousands, ten thousands, hundred thousands, millions, ten millions, and so forth.

One student asked, "Are there other number systems?" "Well, I have heard of the binary system," responded one member. Rex decided to move ahead on his own, but the others in the group wanted to explore the binary system in more depth. Gloria pointed out that the binary system is based on the number 2. It has only two numbers, 0 and 1.

For example, the number 11010 in the binary system is $2^0 + 2^1 + 2^2 + 2^3 + 2^4$ that equals 1 + 2 + 4 + 8 + 16 which is equal to 21 in the decimal system. Modern calculating machines are based primarily on the binary system since the numbers 1 and 0 can represent on and off positions and are capable of recoding large numbers in a split second electronically. The learning group was motivated to explore the binary system in more depth and also extended their thinking to other number systems such as the quinary system based on the number 5. A light went on and learning was extended. Singular study by each group member might not have raised the question regarding other number systems. Nevertheless, Rex, who opted out of the group at the outset, did not benefit by the group work.

STUDENT PORTFOLIO ASSESSMENT AND EVALUATION

The assessment and evaluation of a student portfolio, or any other portfolio, are based on the evidence as related to the question regarding whether or not the evidence within the portfolio has met the purposes/standards/requirements set forth in the portfolio at the outset of its implementation. The literature varies somewhat as to how this question should be answered. A logical answer to the question tends to focus on how the student provides evidence and just how the expressed experiences added to the learning purposes set forth at the outset. Not only should the learning experiences be underscored, but various artifacts and examples of learning outcomes should be noted.

That is, examples and artifacts should be included in the portfolio that support the 'claim' of learning gained in the specific area of the student's interest. Specific knowledge and skills learned during the completion of the portfolio must be noted. The question as to whether or not the mentioned experiences were directly focused on the learning expectations should be discussed using product examples of course and other artifacts that give evidence of the work required.

The question of whether or not the experience undertaken by the student led to new learning might be addressed by the insertion of how the learning was applied (or could be applied) in practice. For example, a student who took a course in the 'new math' might include an example of its application in using a new number system in electronic accounting or a lesson plan showing an example of clock arithmetic, whereby the key math characteristics of associative and distributive mathematical laws are utilized.

What evidence is shown in the student portfolio that 'growth' has taken place? After all, this is a primary purpose of the portfolio. Has the student set forth any examples of learning growth through the application of self-evaluation? What artifacts might be inserted in the portfolio as evidence that personal assessment and evaluation of the product have taken place? Before and after examples of written reports, test scores in a course, applications of the learning achieved, and comments relative to how the new learning can be helpful in future courses and activities are such improvement documentations.

The final presentation of a student's portfolio varies widely depending of its inclusiveness, time consumption, purposes, and requirements. In any case, an 'attractive,' well organized, and written portfolio is considered important in most portfolio program. *Navigation* is the term used that centers on how 'easy' it is to use the portfolio. How organized is the product? Does the information in the portfolio move logically from one content section to another? Is a table of contents with page numbers appropriate and utilized in the final product? Is the portfolio logically organized as opposed to being simply a collection of information and examples? Is the portfolio error free in regard to correct grammar, spelling, and required content?

STUDENT PORTFOLIOS AND THEIR BENEFITS FOR SCHOOL ADMINISTRATION

Most thought is given to how student portfolios help the student in the learning process. Nevertheless, such portfolios hold many benefits for school administrators related to providing positive support for quality teaching, engaging students in the instructional procedures, and opening communication channels between students, teachers, and the administrators of the school. More specifically, student portfolios can serve accountability reporting, program evaluations, and other administrative decisions affecting student curricular programming. Reportedly, the use of student portfolios has been cited as being beneficial in the administrative areas of curriculum development/improvement and assessment.

Specific uses of portfolios in preparation programs at the higher education level include just being a part of a specific course requirement. In some cases, a student portfolio is required in lieu of a final course examination or part of the requirement for an administrative internship or other practicum activities. In some cases, a portfolio is required at the outset of the graduate student's program experiences. Artifacts of the student's work at the outset of the degree or licensing program are recorded at the outset of the student's admission to the program and assessed and evaluated at the time of program completion. In fact, some administrator programs have used portfolios as part of the admission requirement.

THE IMPLEMENTATION OF STUDENT PORTFOLIOS IN PRACTICE

In 2004, 63 departments of educational administration were surveyed with regard to the extent that student portfolios were being used in their

Table 1.2 Programs Using Student Learning Portfolios in Preparation Programs in Educational Administration in 2004

Study sample	90
Respondents	63 (70%)
Respondents using portfolios	57 (90%)
Degree/Certification	Percent of Subgroup Using Portfolios (%)
Master's degree	89.5
Educational Specialist (EdS)	36.8
EdD degree	26.3
PhD degree	31.6
Certification/Licensing	47.4

preparation programs. Of the 63 departments, 90% of them were using portfolios in five different degree and licensing programs. Specifically, 89.5% of the departments were using portfolios in their master's degree programs (see table 1.2).

At the time of this survey, the five leading uses of student learning portfolios in administrative preparation programs in rank order were for the administrative internship (73.7%); as part of a course requirement (52.6%); in lieu of the comprehensive examination for a degree (47.45%); a method of evaluating student skills at various times during student preparation or at the close of a specific program (42.1%); and as a means for reporting and/or assessing fieldwork or other practicum (36.8%).

It is clear that the leading three uses of portfolios in 2004 were related to a specific course and/or field requirements. Portfolio uses for the purposes of student admission, program continuation, achievement of state requirements, or research topic exploration were much less significant. For example, only 10.6% of the institutions used student portfolios to assess entry year performance for the purpose of deciding continuation in the program or to assess achievement of certain state standards.

ATTEMPTS TO DETERMINE THE EXTENT OF PORTFOLIO UTILIZATION TODAY

Attempts to determine the current usage of student portfolios in degree programs in any subject area are most difficult. In 2020, we were able to find little information relative to current portfolio utilization at the K–12 school level or in degree programs in higher education. In 2013, Bryant and Chittum authored an article titled "ePortfolio Effectiveness: A(n Ill-Fated) Search for Empirical Support." It is beyond the scope of chapter 1 to detail the information provided by this journal article; however, we do recommend its reading even though it was published seven years ago.

Bryant and Chittum conclude the article by stating:

> Although ePortfolio research is increasingly evident in the literature, a transition toward empirical assessment of their impact on student outcome is needed. It is time for the research to make this crucial shift so that ePortfolios can either attain their full potential, or valuable time and resources can be allotted to a more worthy cause. (p. 196)

One survey centered on the uses of portfolios in the administrator preparation program. The participating universities reported that portfolios were part of their course requirement (52%); were used in lieu of a comprehensive examination (47.4%); were used as a requirement for the administrative internship (73.7%); were used for fieldwork and other administrative practicum (36.6%); were used to evaluate students in relation to admission requirements (10.6%); were used to decide continuation in the administration program (10.6%); were used as part of the state's requirements (10.6%); and were used to explore topics for the master's and doctoral dissertation topics (5.3%). This informal survey was not scientific, but its results did give some information regarding the nature of portfolio uses and the extent to which portfolios were being used in administrator preparation programs within the nation.

Portfolios have been shown to be useful in helping teachers and administrators show students the primary importance of work quality. A student's best work is of paramount importance in learning and educational progress. A related benefit of portfolios is vested in the fact that a student's quality performance is of considerable value for enhancing the performance of others. That is, quality work can be recorded and saved for referencing in future work by the administration, teachers, and other students. Additionally, the important characteristics of collaboration, communication, critical thinking, and other positive traits can accompany the planning, development, and implementation of a portfolio program.

PORTFOLIOS AND THEIR PLANNING AND IMPLEMENTATION: A COLLABORATIVE PROGRAM

Some documentation recommendations may be somewhat surprising even to those who do teach. For example, various recommendations for documentation include not only courses taught and instructional methods utilized, but recommend that enrollment figures, syllabi, lesson plans, evaluation procedures, reading lists, homework requirements, tests that are implemented, instructional materials utilized, technology used in teaching, teacher load information, class sizes, and related extracurricular assignments be included in the teaching portfolio. It is recommended that the following secondary and elementary teacher load formulas be used to calculate *teacher load data* that can be included in the teacher's teaching portfolio (Douglass 1950; Norton and Bria 1992).

The question might be raised as to whether or not 'group thinking' has any advantages over the thinking of one individual. Studies by William Bombeck (1973) and others have shown that group thinking arrives at better answers than singular thinking. Bombeck's doctoral dissertation revealed that 'thinking groups' arrived at better solutions than individual respondents in all but one instance when several groups and several individuals were involved in problem situations. Consumer Guide (1993, December) supported the use of portfolios in relation to making administrative decisions. Yet, there does exist certain reservations about using student portfolios in administrative matters.

In all too many cases, students are ill-prepared to perform the in-depth work required for the administrative decisions at hand. The practical experience of most students is limited and the problems encountered in administrative work call for thinking/experience far beyond that needed for problem resolution. Students who have limited proficiency in the use of the English language tend to encounter problems that require such expertise. Students commonly work on different tasks. Therefore, only one portfolio might be available that is judged by only one person. The singular results tend to be insufficient for placing any credibility on the portfolio results.

STUDENT PORTFOLIOS DO HAVE PROBLEMS AMID CONTROVERSIAL ISSUES

It is difficult to find a school program offering a school policy that is not encircled by both supporters and non-supporters. Debates in the area of student portfolio programs are present as well. Planning, implementing, and administering a student portfolio program within a school are difficult at best. First of all, the 'added work' of student portfolios placed on the teacher's already heavy load becomes troublesome. In some cases, only a few students commonly are involved in the portfolio program, and therefore it can become a before- and after-school program event. Additionally, the large majority of the teaching faculty is not experienced or is poorly prepared to assume the teacher's role in such programs. As a result, student portfolios can be poorly done and have little to give toward program/course improvement. When finished, therefore, many are just filed away and ultimately forgotten.

The initiation of a portfolio program is time-consuming and, as previously mentioned, becomes an added work assignment for a teacher's already heavy workload. Funding for such 'new programs' is not readily available. Keeping abreast of each student's portfolio progress and reading all the portfolios for assessment and evaluation purposes generally becomes burdensome. When the portfolios are seldom used, especially when they are poorly done, attention to the program fades over time. Well, then, are student portfolios really worth the time and effort it takes to complete them? The answer is a positive 'yes.' The foregoing comments underscore the important need for school leaders to re-think and revise the problem of teacher load. As previously noted, specific teacher load formulas have been developed for bringing equity into the problem of teacher burnout and early resignation from a teaching profession.

Final standardized tests are easily scored and graded. Results on standardized tests can be used for a variety of administrative purposes. On the other hand, supporters of student portfolios contend that they are for students and not administrators. They do have important implications for the classroom and program effectiveness. In any case, student portfolios, like any other curricular activity provided by the school, will contribute effectively to the school program to the extent that it is planned, implemented, and carried out by knowledgeable and skilled teacher/administrative personnel. Nevertheless, student portfolios hold the most significant benefit for the school when teachers and student relationships are focused on learning programs in the best interests of student learning.

Several problems that are being encountered in the use of student learning portfolios tend to center on the following seven problem: (1) lack of faculty time for supervising and evaluating the portfolio program responsibilities;

(2) lack of student time for reporting periodically on progress; (3) lack of faculty incentives for guiding, advising, and evaluating; (4) lack of faculty interest in the use of portfolios; (5) lack of agreement regarding quality guidelines for portfolio utilization; (6) lack of agreement regarding quality guidelines for their use; (7) lack of faculty agreement regarding the place of portfolios in the curricular program; and (8) too many student complaints concerning their use.

WHAT IS THE STATUS OF STUDENT PORTFOLIOS IN SCHOOL PROGRAMS NATIONALLY?

Certainly, portfolios are not new to the profession of education or to other professions such as architecture, business, law, engineering, art, and sales. Architects organize samples of their drawings and work history for the purpose of gathering consideration for work interviews, providing evidence of work quality for consideration as part of the screening process in contractual competition, or documenting the attainment of job requirements for personal advancement and merit evaluations. In the field of education, portfolios historically have been used for such purposes as internship logs, field project journals, activity mappings, specific course learnings, and as a means to reveal personal growth and development.

Portfolios used in student teaching commonly include records of class curricular contents, student learning activities, instructional methodology, and other information used for student counseling and self-assessment and evaluation. Some evidence has shown that the student portfolio is replacing the use of personal resumes which have been used for job applications for many years. Although the personal resume most often does include a statement of career goals, a summary of work history, and a list of references, the student portfolio also includes a number of artifacts that create a showcase of documents representing the applicant's best work and accomplishments. Not only are the various job positions and where the student's experience took place stated in the portfolio, but the applicant's best work and accomplishment are underscored.

Student portfolio information not only indicates the positions held by the applicant but emphasizes how the stated purposes were accomplished. Evidence for such accomplishments are supported not only by the references included in the portfolio, but the artifacts and samples of work give specific evidence of what was successful in the work activities of the student. From this perspective, a student portfolio represents the major purposes of the course or program activity in question but also presents evidence as to what was done by the student to achieve the stated goals and objectives.

It is difficult to describe the status of K–12 schools nationally due to the problems created by the virus pandemic. However, before the event of Covid-19, evidence was present that some high schools had initiated portfolios to assess and evaluate student academic progress. In one California school program, for example, the portfolio program was initiated for the purposes of preparing students for college and for assessing whether or not students were acquiring the knowledge and skills needed to succeed after graduation.

One school district in California had established the implementation, completion, and defense performances of a portfolio as mandatory for graduation. The learning portfolio was required along with the completion of standard course credits and other credits such as job shadowing, internships, and community service. At this point and time, it is not certain about the status of portfolio use in schools nationally. It would seem to be especially beneficial to determine if portfolio programs have increased or declined in view of the program changes that have been made in school programs including the closing of school programs altogether.

Chapter 1 has focused on the nature of student/teacher portfolios and if and how portfolios are being used in education and other professions nationally. We ask our readers to think for a moment about the state of the portfolio utilization in their work/life experiences. For example, are portfolios used in any way in the position(s) in which you have experienced? If so, just what have been the primary purposes of their implementation? On a scale of 1 being low and 5 being high, how important/effective has the portfolio program been in your work settings?

In chapter 2, we set forth data and information relating to the use and value of portfolios, primarily as related to positions in professional education. Chapter 2 continues to center on the extended utilization of portfolios in other educational practices and in the world of business.

Preceding the entry of the chapter's Key Chapter Ideas and Recommendations, we include an example of a comprehensive portfolio's requirements for a degree program in educational administration. The example is not to be viewed as a model for all graduate student portfolios in administration, but rather as an example that was being used in a major university within the United States. Although we do not list the name of the university, we have received permission to use the following information and to make minor changes that might be necessary for making it more related to university programs across the nation. It was our thought that such an entry would be helpful to the reader who could examine the format and contents of an administrative portfolio to be completed for credit within one national university.

KEY CHAPTER IDEAS AND RECOMMENDATIONS

- Contemporary student grading practices fall short of helping to understand what actually was learned or not learned during the time of program and grading activities.
- Although the contention is often expressed that the student's interests and needs are of high importance, it appears to be seldom practiced in K–12 learning program practices.
- Grading criteria range widely in K–12 school settings, making it impossible to tell what it means to receive a grade of A.
- A student portfolio has been defined as an organized goal-driven documentation of one's professional growth, achievement, and experiences.
- A quality student portfolio can serve the student, the teacher(s), and the school in efforts to make the school a learning center.
- The planning and drafting of a quality portfolio begin with a focus on learning and its related purposes.
- Portfolio statements related to the student's learning must be accompanied by evidence that demonstrates the fact that new knowledge and skills have indeed taken place.
- In the end, an effective student portfolio will show in detail what the student really knows and how he or she is able to apply that knowledge.
- During troubled times, such as the virus pandemic, a safe environment for the student to learn is a top priority.
- Collaboration and group decision-making can be enhanced when students are encouraged to work and think together.

- Time will tell whether or not the concept of student portfolios will be promoted to the extent that a student's involvement in the learning program is increased and self-development indeed is being practiced.

REFERENCES

Barrett, H. C. (2020). The Research on Portfolios in Education. From the web: electronicportfolios.org/AL/Research.html

Bombeck, W. (1973). Group Decision Making vs. Individual Decision Making. Unpublished doctoral dissertation, Arizona State University, Tempe, AZ.

Bryant, L. H., and Chittum, J. R. (2013, November 2). ePortfolio Effectiveness: A(n ill-Fated) Search For Empirical Support. *International Journal of ePortfolio*, 3, November 2, 189–98.

Danielson, C., and Abrutyn, L. (1997, June 1). *Introduction to Using Portfolios in the Classroom*, 1st Edition. Association of Supervision and Curriculum Development. Alexandria, VA.

Douglass, H. R. (1951). The 1950 Revision of the Douglass High School Teaching Load Formula. *NASSP Bulletin*, 35, 13–24.

Evans, S. M. (1995). *Professional Portfolios: Documenting and Presenting Performance Excellence*. Virginia Beach, VA: Teacher's Little Secrets.

Hopkinson, A. (2017). High school Turing to student portfolios to assess academic progress, ESource. Highlighting Strategies for Student Success. On the web: https://sourcelorg/2017/high-schools-Turning-to-student-portfolios-to-assess-academic-progress-580/47

Kelly, M. (2019, November 14). Getting Started with Student Portfolios. ThoughtCo., Resources for Educators, Dotdash Publishing Family. Resources for Educators, New York, NY.

Norton, M. S. (2004). *The HR Director in Arizona: A Research Study:* Tempe: Arizona State University Division of Educational Administration & Policy Studies.

Norton, M. S., and Bria, R. (1992). Toward an Equitable Measure of Elementary School Teacher Load. *Record in Educational Administration and Supervision*, 13(1), 62–66.

Chapter 2

The World of Portfolios

How Portfolios Are Used, Assessed, and Evaluated

Primary Chapter Goal: To continue the focus on the many uses of portfolios for student learning and growth, teacher professional growth, and benefits to administrative management.

MORE EXAMPLES OF LEARNING PORTFOLIOS AND HOW THEY ARE ASSESSED AND EVALUATED

The common definition of a portfolio is that it is a collection of evidence about something of importance. It has a specific purpose and all of the information/items in the portfolio are directly related to the purpose set forth. The items in the portfolio most often are referred to as 'evidence' that lends to the purpose and supports the fact that the purpose has been accomplished. Thus, professional growth, learning knowledge, professional advancement, and personal experience are specific evidence that a purpose has or has not been achieved. A *working portfolio* is one designed to be used in the classroom or completed digitally or through various homeschooling strategies.

Professional growth is evidenced in the results of academic work that has been successfully learned and in one's ability to apply in practice the knowledge that has been achieved. Professional growth is reflected in one's ability to implement the leadership knowledge that has been learned over time. In addition, professional growth is evidenced in the way the individual uses the learning to improve leadership practices.

A *leadership portfolio* contains evidence of one's ongoing improvement as a leader in the practice. One's uniqueness as a leader is informed by the contents in the portfolio that report the ongoing improvement of one's work with others and how he or she shows a broader understanding of the leadership qualities that are possessed. There is a growing understanding of the knowledge and values that have led to one's increasing improvement as a leader in practice.

Various artifacts, written papers for administration requirements, readings, field experiences, self-evaluation activities, and one's work successes and unfortunate errors serve to broaden one's understanding of self and the ever-changing world in which we live. What the person learns about self, in turn, will serve as a continuing guide for leadership and decision matters that invariably will be faced in administrative practice.

A RUBRIC SCORING GUIDE FOR ONE TYPE OF A PORTFOLIO

The assessment and evaluation of certain types of student portfolios can be completed by the use of a scoring rubric. An *assessment portfolio* is a portfolio that presents evidence of student learning and documents that the student has or has not achieved the knowledge and skills necessary for meeting a program's standards and objectives. Study.com (no date) suggests a rather

Table 2.1 Rubric Guide for a Writing Portfolio Assessment

Score	When the Student
4	Includes a piece of work for each item on the checklist that clearly meets the criteria suggested; writes short paragraph about each item, weaving a connection between the pieces and describing what knowledge/skills were learned; shows reflection about his or her thinking and learning over time.
3	Includes a piece of work for each item on the checklist; writes a short paragraph about each item; is somewhat reflective of how his or her thinking has changed.
2	Includes a piece of work for each item; writes something about each piece.
1	Includes a piece of work for most items; writes little about the pieces of work.
0	Does not complete the task or gives information that has nothing to do with the work chosen.

'simple' rubric for doing so. In the case of a writing portfolio, table 2.1 is one example of such an evaluation guide.

A *Rubric Scoring Guide* serves to 'grade' a portfolio's contents during an assessment and evaluation process. Each entry within the portfolio is graded using a scoring chart for such content and inclusions as purpose, quality, knowledge gained, and so on.

EXAMPLES OF OTHER RUBRICS FOR SCORING STUDENT PORTFOLIOS

Vandervelde (2001–2018) set forth excellent examples of other rubrics for assessing and evaluating a student. Eight specific criteria were identified including: (1) selection of artifacts; (2) description text; (3) reflective commentary; (4) citations; (5) navigation; (6) usability and assessability: text elements, layout, and color; (7) writing conventions; and (8) multimedia elements. Each of the criteria is to be rated as being unsatisfactory, emerging, proficient, or exemplary. For example, within the criteria of selection of artifacts, if the selection of artifacts and work samples do not relate to the purpose of the portfolio, an unsatisfactory rating is recorded.

On the other hand, if all artifacts and work samples are clearly and directly related to the purposes of the portfolio and a wide variety of artifacts is included, the highest rating of exemplary is given to the selection criteria. We recommend Vandervelde's article as an excellent example of portfolio scoring (see chapter references).

SUMMARY OF HOW STUDENT PORTFOLIOS CAN BE MOST HELPFUL WHEN USED IN THE CLASSROOM, WHEREVER THAT MIGHT BE

The primary benefit of portfolios is their use by students and teachers in the regular classroom. During school closures, such as the times when schools are closed due to the Covid-19 pandemic, student learning through the development of portfolios can be of great value.

First and foremost, portfolios can serve the purpose of assessing and evaluating the learning status of the student. What the student actually has learned and the extent to which the student has mastered the work are reflected in the quality of the student's portfolio. The student portfolio becomes a way that progress is measured and also identifies any 'weaknesses' of the student's learning and what is needed to close the learning gaps left open by the student. It is evident that the assessment and evaluation of the student's portfolio must be ongoing as opposed to a product that is reviewed at the end of the activity or at the close of the school year.

In some cases, group involvement in the assessment and evaluation might be implemented by using well-known group strategies used in Brainstorming, the Nominal Group Technique, or the Delphi Technique. *Brainstorming* is a participative strategy whereby a group of individuals meets and voices spontaneous ideas relative to a matter of interest that requires a solution or evaluation assessment. An idea expressed by one member might conjure up an extended idea by another member that ultimately leads to a possible solution to the matter at hand.

Authorities point out that student homework, quizzes, and tests most commonly show only what 'learning' has been achieved at one point and time. On the contrary, student portfolios are best when they indicate what the student has learned and what progress has been achieved over a longer period of time. For example, the quality of a student's writing that is assessed at the outset of his or her activity and then only once during the activity at hand is insufficient for evaluating the progress that has occurred over a lengthy period of time. That is, it might not demonstrate the student's best work.

THE NOMINAL GROUP TECHNIQUE

The *Nominal Group Technique* is a decision-making or problem-solving process used by group members who participate in person or by digital methods. Everyone in the group submits his or her input relative to the solutions or answers needed. Each idea is posted and discussed. Duplicate ideas are eliminated and the activities continue until the members agree on the best ideas or solutions.

THE *DELPHI TECHNIQUE*

The *Delphi Technique* requires a group of 'experts' to give their opinions for several questions relative to a current or future problem/matter. Several rounds of questions are posed until a statistical response of the group is reached. The *technique* involves a group of 'experts' and an important topic for which these experts give their opinions. Several rounds of questionnaires are sent to the participating members, and answers are posed by them in each case. Ultimately, a statistical response(s) is reached and announced as the best answer or solution to the matter at hand. The time factor for the Delphi process is somewhat lengthy but is highly beneficial for certain matters such as thoughts about the educational knowledge and skills needed by students in the future.

Effective learning not only requires the acquisition of knowledge and skills, but it also requires information as to the student's ability to understand and apply the data, principles, and applications of the learning. This transfer of learning looms important for determining the success of the student who hopes to be successful in business practices, industrial activities, economic, and other areas of the world of work. Such information not only is important for individual life activities, but looms as important evidence for determining the academic progress of the student in relation to the completion of high school graduation and potential for success in entering and completing a college degree.

Education authorities and others historically have reiterated the paramount importance of cooperation, communication, and collaboration. Each of these three characteristics has been underscored by many persons as being essential for success today as well as in the future. Yet, these characteristics have tended to be important but ineffectively practiced in the modern world. *Group thinking* is a strategy whereby more than one person serves in a discussion or in reaching a solution or best answer to a question or problem at hand. Virtually every 'authority' on portfolios has contended that collaboration is the sine qua non of successful planning, execution, and assessment of an effective educational program. Student portfolios have the potential of improving this situation.

IN TROUBLED TIMES, COMMUNICATION TENDS TO BECOME PROBLEMATIC

Without question, an effective program of student portfolios can serve the effectiveness of student, teacher, and parent communication. In reality today, parents learn about the status and progress of their child periodically via the distribution of the periodic report card. What is learned about the student's status most commonly is a grade of A through F or 1 through 5. Just what the student has learned or what growth has been realized is not clear. If the grade improves or regresses, reason(s) why is never clear. The student's and parent's knowledge of the growth that has occurred over a period of time can be revealed by way of effective portfolio development. Specific learning 'products' are available for examination, and product quality can be readily examined.

Thus, parent activity, set forth in the educational program, can be identified and considered in the future learning program for the student. When parents are not adequately informed about the child's learning program and status, they are at ends relative to what they might do to help improve their child's weaknesses and foster their future success.

BEST WORKS PORTFOLIOS: SHOWING THE HIGHEST LEVEL OF A STUDENT'S ACHIEVEMENT

Think of a time when you, your parents, teachers, and friends expressed the belief that something that you accomplished was the most rewarding work, activity, or performance of your life to date. Most likely, you have never forgotten about it. You or your parents might have the work placed in a frame and put on the dining room wall. Or perhaps you pasted it onto a photo book or perhaps put it in your student portfolio

A *quality portfolio* is clearly defined by purpose, procedures, personnel roles and their responsibilities, and the involvement of students and parents in planning and implementing the portfolio program. Portfolios that display one's best work give the individual a chance for enjoying their best work and gaining a sense of accomplishment that results in making the many efforts of work enjoyable and more worthwhile. It fosters a positive attitude toward learning as well as making a meaningful contribution to the positive climate of the home or classroom of the school. As noted by Danielson and Abrutyn (1997), "The choices (that students make) define them as students and as learners. In making their selections, students illustrate what they believe to be important about their learning, what they value, and want to show to others" (p. 3).

ASSESSMENT PORTFOLIOS: DEMONSTRATING THE STUDENT'S MASTERY OF LEARNINGS

Indiana University (2016) summarized the assessment guidance for student portfolios. Emphasis was given to 'assessment criteria' and their importance in providing clear evidence that the student has mastered the course learning outcomes and competencies that the course requires. Six specific criteria are assessed: (1) sources of learning; (2) demonstration of learning; (3) evidence of learning; (4) mastering knowledge and skills; (5) reflection on learning; and (6) presentation.

Each of these criteria is rated by use of a scoring rubric. For example, number 3 of the criteria, *evidence of learning*, requires that the portfolio should demonstrate that the experience has resulted in learned competencies and that the learning is aligned with course learning knowledge and skills. That is, the portfolio information must tie the learning experiences to sound educational theory. Thusly, the criterion of *mastering knowledge and skills* must be demonstrated in the learning outcomes and shown that they can be applied in practice.

As would be expected, the University of Wisconsin (Vandervelde 2001–2018) used eight different criteria for assessment purposes, including: (1) selection of artifacts; (2) descriptive texts; (3) reflective commentary; (4) citations; (5) navigation; (6) usable and assessable: text elements, layout, and color; (7) writing conventions; and (8) multimedia elements (optimal). As an example, the criterion of *navigation* focuses on various parts of the portfolio that are labeled, clearly organized, and easily located throughout the portfolio.

In the early 1990s, academic achievement was assessed increasingly by the use of norm-referenced multiple-choice tests. The criticism of this kind of testing comes from the belief that such tests did not reveal what the student had learned; a different methods of assessing student learning had to be implemented that revealed what the student had learned over a specific period of time and whereby learning strengths and weaknesses could be identified. Something that would reveal the student's knowledge and skills required for some important objective such as movement from elementary to secondary school, high school graduation, or entrance into college.

The primary purpose of the assessment portfolio then is to present evidence of student learning that documents that the student has or has not achieved the knowledge necessary for meeting the program objectives. As noted previously, the program objective might be to move from elementary school grade to another higher grade, to move from elementary school to secondary school, or graduate from high school. In each of these cases, the content of the portfolio must be of high quality and possess validity and reliability. It is common for the student to show his or her best work in an assessment portfolio since 'high stake results' are likely to be involved in the outcome.

PORTFOLIO ASSESSMENT AT THE ELEMENTARY SCHOOL LEVEL

An article by Gelfer and Perkins (1995), published 25 years ago, centered on portfolio assessment at the elementary school level. Although dated, this quality article is unique in many respects and chapter 2 would be unfulfilled without the following reference. In brief the following four statements, set forth in the article, underscore its focus: What characteristics should an assessment procedure have that will focus parent/teacher communication? What assessment approach allows for these essential characteristics? What do portfolios look like? How is a portfolio organized? Note the emphasis on teacher/parent communication.

Make note of the fact that a student portfolio is a meaningful collection of the student's work that *exemplifies students' interests*, *attitudes*, *ranges of skills*, and *development* over a period of time. Isn't the focus on the student's interests and needs just what education authorities have been calling for over the last several decades? The PAP model (Portfolio Assessment Preparation Model) is initiated by two important steps: step 1: orientation/overview for teachers and step 2: workshops for teachers and parents. The purposes and goals of the portfolio along with the assessment process are discussed. In step 2, in-service workshops for teachers and parent orientation sessions are implemented (Gelfer and Perkins 1995).

For the most part, parent, teacher, and student responses to the implementation and execution of the PAP model were positive. For example, one parent commented, "I am very happy I can play a part in reporting my child's grading." A teacher replied, "Initially it was time consuming but it fell into place and conferences went smoothly." A student commented: "I have really grown." Keep in mind that chapters 1 and 2 are centered on the common problems of grading in elementary and secondary schools and ways in which grading might take place more effectively. The implementation of portfolio programs is one primary way in which grading can be more meaningful and beneficial.

A REVIEW QUIZ FOR CHAPTERS 1 AND 2

As opposed to a chapter summary, the following chapter quiz is being used for the purpose of summarizing the major information presented in chapters 1 and 2. In this case, considerable review/reading is required in order to find the 'best' response for each statement presented.

Directions: For each of the fifteen entries, complete the sentence by re-reading the sentence as presented in the chapter. For example, if the statement began as follows: "The contents of a portfolio must be . . .," the answer would be "of high quality, valid, and reliable."

Quiz Statements

1. Basing a student's grade on 'what was learned' commonly is undermined by . . .
2. The working portfolio is especially designed to be used in the classroom regardless of whether . . .
3. Periodic assessment and evaluation of the student's portfolio . . .
4. Most commonly, a student portfolio is a collection of . . .
5. The contents of the student's portfolio include . . .
6. The three Ps of a student portfolio are . . .
7. A student's portfolio is a collection of the . . .
8. Working portfolios commonly center on whether the student is currently working and . . .
9. Display portfolios are ones in which . . .
10. Rather than stressing the importance of doing your own work . . .
11. Studies by William Bombeck and others have shown that . . .
12. The assessment and evaluation of certain types of portfolios can be evaluated by the use of . . .
13. Effective learning not only requires the acquisition of knowledge and skills . . .

14. The primary purpose of the assessment of portfolios is to . . .
15. The primary purpose of an assessment portfolio then is to . . .

Select the answers to the foregoing statements from the following list. Look for the best answer in each case. It is expected that you will have to return to the chapter content to complete the quiz. The answers to the 15 statements are included in the listing that follows, but, of course, are not in alphabetical order. That is, the answer to question #1 above, is not letter 'a.'

Listing of the Various Answers to the Quiz

a. present evidence of student learning.
b. purpose, purpose, and purpose.
c. students, teachers, administrators, and others set forth displays of most important work accomplishments.
d. the actual learning takes place in the school classroom completed digitally or through various homeschooling.
e. open classrooms have been instrumental in purposely promoting groups of students to study and learn together.
f. present evidence of student learning.
g. that serve to assess and evaluate work completed for a specific course.
h. a scoring rubric.
i. what learning is taking place that enhances his or her knowledge and competency for the work.
j. group thinking arrives at better answers than singular thinking.
k. other teacher behavioral traits that influence the teacher's judgment of the active learning outcomes.
l. the academic work of a student accompanied by various examples that show the quality level of the student's work, the progress that the student has made during a specific time period, the extent to which the student dealt with the required standards, and other quality measures.
m. *by* purpose, procedures, and supervisory/teacher roles and responsibilities.
n. documentation of special activities, publications, courses taken, workshop experiences, and other appropriate learned information and skills.
o. but also requires information as to the student's ability to understand and apply the data and principles learned.

ANSWERS TO THE QUIZ

1. The answer to #1 is 'k.' Subjective traits such as student behavior, teacher/pupil relationships, the student's contributions to class discussions/activities, absenteeism, and other affective characteristics of the student tend to influence the grading of a student. Supporters of the portfolio program contend that the assessment and evaluation procedures used in 'grading' portfolios reduce subjectivity due to the purpose and objectivity of the portfolios process.
2. The answer to #2 is 'd.' Although classroom learning is of great importance, digital learning, homeschooling, field experiences, and other school community learning activities suit the purposes of the student learning portfolio. This fact is one important reason why student portfolios are well suited in case of major problems when schools must be closed.
3. The answer to #3 is 'f.' Since purposes and standards are given much attention at the outset of establishing a portfolio program, the strategies for assessing and evaluating the student's learning program are facilitated. Subjectivity is substantially reduced and objectivity is promoted.
4. The answer to #4 is 'l.' The portfolios show three specific quality characteristics: various examples of the student's work, the extent to which the examples show the quality of the work, and the extent to which the examples show if the required program standards have been met.
5. The answer to #5 is 'm.' In quality student portfolios, purpose, procedures, and the roles of teachers are clearly defined.
6. The answer to #6 is 'n.' The documentation of the specific activities in which the student was engaged, courses taken, field experiences, publications, and other evidence of learning are included in the contents of a student portfolio.
7. The answer to #7 is 'b,' purpose, purpose, and purpose. It is clear that the goals and objectives of a student's portfolio program serve to guide the student's curricular program. Standards that accompany a particular goal among the primary factors that are assessed and evaluated in each student portfolio.
8. The answer to #8 is 'g.' The assessment and evaluation of the student portfolio is the sine qua non of a portfolio's quality. It represents a positive answer to the many problems of grading faced by the everyday

classroom teachers. Special procedure for completing the assessment and evaluation procedures do vary. Nevertheless, objectivity, as opposed to subjectivity, is the guiding characteristic for those persons participating in the process.

9. The answer to #9 is 'c.' That is, when the student is working, it is important to know if that experience is enhancing his or her knowledge and competency for the work.
10. The answer to #10 is 'e.' Important work accomplishment are important outcomes of effective portfolio programs. Thus, students and others take part in the displaying of work illustrations that demonstrate important work accomplishments.
11. The answer to #11 is 'j.' Closed classrooms and individual learning have lost their favor over the past few years. Rather, collaboration and cooperation currently are being viewed as being best for all learners. Group work, as opposed to individual homework, is being favored. Student interest and 'enjoyment' in the learning process are enhanced.
12. The answer to #12 is 'i.' Available research study results (Bombeck 1973) have shown that group decision-making is better overall than when one person makes the decision.
13. The answer to #13 is 'h.' Object rubrics can be devised for evaluating student portfolios that reduces the subjectivity that is revealed in many instances in the common grading system of As to Fs or other number grading methods.
14. The answer to #14 is 'o.' Knowledge is important, but the ability to apply this knowledge constitutes the sine qua non of the portfolio process.
15. The answer to #15 is 'a.' When all is said and done, what the student has learned is referenced in the student's portfolio. This contention includes the point that what is not learned also is determined by an effective portfolio assessment. Nevertheless, both what is learned and what has not been learned hold important considerations for the next steps in the student's learning program and life pursuits.

YOUR QUIZ SCORE

15 to 13 correct is *Exemplary*
12 to 9 correct is *Proficient*

8 to 5 correct is *Emerging*
4 to 0 correct is *Unacceptable*

A CHAPTER SUMMARY STATEMENT

The primary purpose of chapter 2, which was stated at the outset of the chapter, centered on the comprehensive concept of the nature of student portfolios and their value in assessing and evaluating the student portfolio at special times exemplified by the current virus pandemic facing the nation and the world. The purpose included the potential for implementing portfolio programs for students in view of the fact that the nation's schools had faced closure for many months and student learning had been given to homeschooling for the most part.

The grading of students in grades K–12 during the closing of schools placed additional responsibility on school personnel to find ways to implement some kind of learning strategies that would be effective outside the common classroom. The hope was that such interventions as student portfolios might be one important strategy for continuing student learning for some students. Thus, chapter 1 centered primarily on demonstrating what constituted an effective portfolio program, its purposes and benefits for the learner.

Many portfolios include lengthy programs such as the completion of a required course or a semester internship. Experiences of this nature can be divided into shortened units that can be assessed and evaluated periodically. Each unit can be examined and the learning progress can be assessed. Early changes commonly result in later program improvements. In any case, choosing the best time for assessing and evaluating a portfolio depends on the purpose at hand. When a unit assessment is utilized, the results can lead to new motivation on the part of the student or find a slippage in the student's program whereby an additional learning activity has to be added to the student's ongoing program.

The component of student involvement and choice is a given for a successful portfolio program. It is of interest to note that, in some programs, students are especially talented at the outset. Being more specific, the student might be as knowledgeable as the teacher in one or more areas of the planned program. Steps in the program planning, therefore, must include the consideration of current knowledge in the course/activity at hand. Work included in the portfolio logically should set forth the plan for continued knowledge with an entry item that demonstrates the student's knowledge at the outset. Such knowledge and skill are not always adequately assessed and therefore duplication of learning is included in the program plans.

In sum, a portfolio is not the easiest 'document' to plan and then complete. In any case, the portfolio must demonstrate the knowledge and skills that the student has accumulated over a specified period of time. Not only are factors such as student improvement demonstrated in an effective portfolio, but other beneficial learning characteristics commonly are discovered in their assessments and evaluations.

For example, what evidence is shown in the portfolio relative to the student's learning style? What strengths and/or weaknesses are discovered in the student's English grammar and written communication that need to be improved or perhaps extended? As pointed out by Evans (1995) many years ago, a portfolio "represents who you are, where you want to go, and how you plan on getting there" (Evans 1995, p. 11).

In chapter 2, attention is directed toward demonstrating how student portfolios can be implemented in times of the virus pandemic, but also can be key learning programs when open school situations are present. Examples of student portfolios are presented and research information relative to learning results are underscored.

For example, the content area of *presentation* would focus on the quality of the portfolio in regard to its completeness and how effectively the content/information is set forth. How well the portfolio is organized and documented in terms of knowledge and learning skills would be assessed. Similarly, the section on *sources of learning* would focus on how well the learning experiences were highly successful and if the information was directly related to the student's course work and portfolio purposes. In addition, the written presentation of the presentation, for an 'exemplary' rating, would include expected institutional requirements and work accomplishments, written clearly with proper grammar, punctuation, and spelling.

KEY CHAPTER IDEAS AND RECOMMENDATIONS

- Professional growth is evidenced in the results of academic work that has been successfully learned and in the ability to implement the leadership knowledge that has been achieved.

- First and foremost, portfolios can serve the purpose of assessing and evaluating the learning status of the student.
- Effective learning not only requires the acquisition of knowledge, but it also requires information as to the student's ability to understand and apply the ideas, principles, and applications of the learning.
- Students define themselves as student learners in their roles of making their portfolio selections that reveal their personal interests and needs.
- The artifacts and work samples set forth in a portfolio must be directly related to the purposes of the portfolio.
- A common definition of a portfolio is that it is a *collection* of *evidence* about something of *importance*. The words *collection*, *evidence*, and *importance* are underlined.
- In education, the need to obtain the involvement of students and parents in their learning program is commonly voiced but seldom practiced. Quality portfolio program activities give those persons and others positive opportunities to be directly involved in the student's learning program.

REFERENCES

Evans, S. M. (1995). *Professional Portfolios: Documenting and Presenting Performance Excellence.* Virginia Beach, VA: Teacher's Little Secrets.

Hopkinson, A. (2017, April 12). High schools turning to student portfolios to assess academic progress. *EdSource: Highlighting Strategies for Student Success.* On the web: https://edsourcelorg/2017/high-schools-turning-to-student-portfolios-to-assess-academic-Progress/580147

Norton, M. S. (2004). *Student Learning Portfolios: How They Are Being Implemented in Educational Administration Preparation Programs. Planning and Changing.* Illinois State University, Normal, Illinois.

Vandervelde, J. (2001–2018). *Examples of Other Rubrics. Schedule of Online Courses, Certificate Programs, and Graduate Degrees.* University of Wisconsin, Stout, Madison, Wisconsin.

Chapter 3

Portfolios with Many Purposes

Primary Chapter Goal: To continue the focus on the purposes of portfolios with consideration to the variety of portfolios that exist including teacher, administrator, and business portfolios. Portfolios for licensing purposes, degree completion, and other leadership roles also are discussed.

Chapters 1 and 2 underscored the fact that there is a wide variety of portfolios, each of which has its specific purposes, content, and assessment directives. Student portfolios, for example, center on student learning primarily in grades K–12. Teachers are directly involved when student portfolios are being planned, implemented, and assessed. However, personal teacher portfolios serve to address the effectiveness of the teacher in the 'classroom' as well as his or her teaching improvement over time.

In the field of education, portfolios have been used for such purposes as specific course learnings, internship logs, field project journals, activity mappings, and as a means to reveal personal growth and development (Norton, 2004). Student portfolios historically have been important tools in student teaching activities such as class lesson content, student activities, instructional methodology, and other data/information that serves toward introspection of self-evaluation and personal growth.

One early study of graduate students in educational administration centered on the use of student portfolios in their preparation programs. More than 90% of the study participants indicated that student portfolios were being used in some manner in their administrator preparation programs.

Portfolios that focus on administrative personnel or ones that serve to address the completion of degrees and licensing for specific administrative positions are of great benefit. Completing a portfolio for the licensing of administrative positions in education is a highly workable solution for meeting the requirements during the Covid-19 pandemic. An example of a portfolio for the licensing of educational administrators and curriculum and supervision personnel is developed in this chapter.

PORTFOLIO DEVELOPMENT AND EVALUATION PROCEDURES FOR EDUCATIONAL ADMINISTRATION INCLUDING CURRICULUM AND SUPERVISION

Give thought to the many problems in trying to complete a licensing program faced by a graduate student during a troublesome time such as the Covid-19 pandemic. Public school closures inhibit the establishment of intern programs in the field and on-campus classes are most commonly closed as well. Long-distance measures such as digital programming and the establishment of portfolio strategies can come to the rescue. An example of a comprehensive portfolio for the development and evaluation procedures for an administrative degree is presented in the following section. This detailed example serves to provide a working 'picture' of a portfolio as opposed to just listing general comments concerning what the contents of a portfolio should contain.

AN EXAMPLE OF A STUDENT PORTFOLIO

The following example of a student portfolio for the completion of a graduate degree and potential administrative licensing is not presented as the model for all such programs but does contain the primary contents of portfolios implemented for degree purposes in educational administration. It is clear that educational administration degree programs differ within the states and thus degree and licensing requirements for various programs do vary.

   THE DEGREE AND LICENSING PORTFOLIO
      DEVELOPMENT AND EVALUATION PROCEDURES
     Educational Administration and Policy Studies
     INTRODUCTION

All students in a master's, principal certification or superintendent certification program in educational administration and policy studies will be expected to complete a portfolio that presents the primary work experiences during the completion of the degree. The portfolio process is supervised by the student's advisor and related members of the department of educational administration. Every student who is admitted to the administrator degree program is expected to attend the orientation session in which the purposes, procedures, and evaluation of the required portfolio are explained.

Portfolio Program Procedures
The portfolio program for the student begins at the outset of his or her admission to the administration degree/certification program. It is an ongoing program that begins with planning sessions with the student's advisor and, as needed, with members of the student's program committee. As previously noted, each student is expected to complete the portfolio program sessions at the outset; these sessions focus on the nature of the portfolio, its contents and format, and the assessment and evaluation procedures that loom important for its satisfactory completion.

The portfolio should draw on each required course of the program. The instructor of any required course may provide formative feedback about a student's portfolio development which is germane to that course. It is the responsibility of the student to solicit this formative feedback. Students may use the standard course portfolio evaluation forms for assessment and evaluation purposes.

Early planning sessions with the student's advisor are essential. The student's portfolio will be evaluated by a committee consisting of the student's advisor and all members of the advisory committee. It recommended that advisement meetings are scheduled with the student's advisor early on in the degree/certification program. Such information sessions will not only save the student's time but will result in fostering a successful portfolio for presentation at the end of the degree program.

Portfolio Contents and Procedures
As previously noted, the development of a student portfolio is ongoing and thus must begin upon admission to the program of administration. In most cases, specific dates and times for advisor/student assessment session are scheduled at the

outset of the program. However, such sessions mostly depend on student needs and assessment progress. Collaboration during the implementation of the portfolio is essential. Not only is the format for the portfolio of considerable importance, but the program of required and elective courses that will be pursued loom important as well. An official program of studies is to be determined and recorded on the official program forms of the department/university and signed by the student, advisor, and other officials according to specified requirements.

Near the close of the student's program of studies, the portfolio document is to be presented in full to the student's advisor. The advisor, along with members of the student's advisory committee, will examine the portfolio in depth and make the determination as to whether it is ready to be presented in its 'final form' to the entire department faculty or other group that has been named to serve in the final evaluation and assessment of the portfolio.

The common procedure of the final assessment and evaluation of the student's portfolio is for the student to present the planning, implementation, and special work activities at the evaluation session. An overview of each entry in the portfolio commonly is discussed, the best work of the student is underscored, and the implications for practice are emphasized. The committee commonly will utilize the department's scoring rubric for evaluating the portfolio/presentation.

In summary, the portfolio presentation should focus on the contents of the portfolio itself. Not only is the knowledge gained from each activity included in the program fully detailed, but a synopsis as to what was actually learned and the important applications of the learning for administrative practice are underscored. Documentation of each content entry is of primary importance. Documentation is evidenced by using examples of the way in which the student met the stated requirements at hand. Samples of the feedback given by the teacher on written papers presented, artifacts that represent the student's presentation(s) of required oral contributions in group activities, and other artifacts that give credibility to the accomplishment of a special curricular program or other learning activity.

PORTFOLIO ASSESSMENT AND EVALUATION

Portfolios of various kinds require an effective strategy for implementing an assessment and evaluation of the final product. Although the 'grading' of the portfolio is ongoing, a rubric that fits the case commonly is implemented in the final portfolio evaluation and assessment process. A copy of the rubric used within the programs of educational administration is included in this chapter. You will note that the rubric contains seven sections in which a score for quality is indicated. Total scores, as given by the individual members of the advisory committee, are averaged. The average score results in a final judgment of satisfactory or unsatisfactory results.

CASES OF UNSATISFACTORY PORTFOLIOS

In some cases, unsatisfactory portfolio results will be judged additionally by the members of the department as a whole, although the members of the original advisory committee do not participate. Once again, the rubric is used by the 'override' committee and its results determine the final judgment of satisfactory or unsatisfactory for the portfolio. This procedure is valid since most members of the department will have had some input/contact with the student's programming during its completion.

An unsatisfactory result leads to the making of major improvements to the portfolio, once again over time. Just what is to be improved is quite likely to be identified by the scoring results of the advisory and department members who assessed and evaluated the first draft of the 'final' portfolio. Experience has shown that the upgrading needed for unsatisfactory portfolio results generally takes one semester or more to correct. This fact underscores the importance of having the best work of the student included in the first draft of the portfolio.

Unsatisfactory portfolio results point out the most common problem that interferes with a quality product, that of effective collaboration, cooperation, and communication. Not only is the completion of an effective portfolio an ongoing work requirement but requires ongoing relationships among and between the student, teacher, and other related members of the students learning program.

The setting of collaboration meetings only as needed has been found to be unsatisfactory. That is, best recommendations call for a regular schedule of student/advisor collaborative sessions whereby the meeting's purpose, meeting's goals and objectives, the assessment of work completed, and the planned agenda for work to be accomplished between now and the next collaboration session are clearly planned and addressed.

A SCORING RUBRIC FOR A COMPLETED PORTFOLIO

The portfolio commonly contains six specific content areas that center on the student's knowledge and leadership skills. In addition, the portfolio assessment considers the inclusiveness of the content of the portfolio. A scoring rubric is applied to each of the major content entries. The scoring scale used for the portfolio in question might use the number 4 to mean an 'exemplary' performance, the number 3 to mean a 'proficient' performance, the number 2 to mean an 'emerging' performance, and the number 1 to mean an 'unacceptable' performance.

Four sections are included in the rubric for 'scoring' the portfolio including: (1) reports most important knowledge and skills from program course work, professional literature, and field experiences; (2) reports most important knowledge and skills related to administrative leadership in the expected roles of administrative supervisor, school assistant principal, and principal; reports on the important leadership responsibilities for instructional programs and curricular provisions; (3) reports on the important administrative role and responsibilities of organizational leadership; and (4) reports on the important role and responsibilities of community leadership and political impacts on school decisions.

Specific questions for each of the four major portfolio performance areas are asked in the assessment instrument. For example, under the major area of organizational leadership, the student is rated using a score of 4 to 1 on the extent to which he or she discussed and gave examples of their learning and growth in that administrative area. It seems clear that the various university programs of educational administration have some commonalities but also have differences in their program content and operations. Thus, the contents and the scoring system of the assessment instrument will tend to differ among university administrator programs.

EXAMPLES OF SCORING RUBRICS FOR STUDENT PORTFOLIOS

It is clear that there are many different types of portfolios, and these differences are defined in the portfolio's contents. A best works portfolio for a student majoring in art is likely to differ substantially from a portfolio of a student majoring in mathematics or in other academic subjects. In some instances, content topics such as selection of artifacts, descriptive text, reflective commentary, citations, navigation, usability and accessibility, text elements, layout, and color, writing conventions, and multimedia elements might be appropriate. In others, such as a specific learning portfolio, such content areas might include sources of learning, demonstration of learning, evidence of learning, and presentation of the final product.

Assessment ratings related to the *mastering of knowledge and skills* are of special importance, although the sources of learning, demonstration of learning, evidence of learning, and reflection on learning sections loom important as well. After all, it is of paramount importance to present evidence that the students have gained the knowledge and skills required by the school standards. Such questions as the following must be addressed: How long has the student worked in order to meet the expected standards for the course? Can the student apply the knowledge gained in practice? What evidence is shown to demonstrate that the student has implemented the self-evaluation strategies that result in added personal growth and development?

The student's oral comments and responses to questions posed are of great importance. General comments such as, "the experience that I had at my school was not only interesting but I really learned a lot" or "I really did not enjoy my class in Algebra 1, but Algebra 2 was different and I learned a lot" are vague and inappropriate. Of most importance is how the presentation in the student's portfolio actually demonstrates that the second algebra experience was purposeful in meeting the requirements of the school's program, the purposes of the portfolio, and the growth in learning that took place during the time that the program was active.

STUDENT PORTFOLIOS, YES, BUT WHAT ABOUT TEACHING PORTFOLIOS?

Evidence has supported the contention that the very best teachers in a school are first to 'demand' opportunities for continuous professional growth. If such opportunities are not provided, these teachers tend to search for positions where self-improvement programs are available and active. Teacher portfolios serve various purposes.

The individual who aspires to become a member of the teaching profession develops a *teaching portfolio* that emphasizes his or her preparation accomplishments, teaching philosophy, and special knowledge and skills. Student teachers have found portfolios of special benefit for demonstrating class lesson content, instructional methods, student activities, and various strategies implemented for assessing student learning. Although such information serves to inform teacher supervisors as to the activities of the student teacher, the portfolio content is invaluable in helping the student and teachers reflect on the lesson programming and its effectiveness in meeting the learning purposes set forth at the outset of a unit or work.

We keep in mind that, as one grows and develops professionally, thoughts about what is good and the importance of purpose tend to change. The term *growth* implies that change has taken place. Therefore, it seems clear that the teacher's portfolio will change. New ideas, educational purposes, student needs, and individual interests do change and the teacher's portfolio should reflect changes as well.

Teaching portfolios have the potential of providing a variety of ways to assess and evaluate teaching. Commonly, teacher performance is decided by a school principal who visits the teacher's classroom during a semester and derives a performance statements that centers on such characteristics as student behavior, learner involvement, and quality of presentation. On the other hand, a teaching portfolio has the potential of demonstrating the teacher's effectiveness in the classroom, providing specific evidence regarding that effectiveness, demonstrating the extent of the teacher's knowledge in the area of instruction, and pointing out both the strengths and weaknesses of the teacher's effectiveness for establishing a learning climate in the classroom.

For example, the content area of *presentation* would focus on the quality of the portfolio in regard to its completeness and how effectively the content/information is set forth. How well the portfolio is organized and documented in terms of knowledge and learning skills would be assessed. Similarly, the section on *sources of learning* would focus on how well the learning experiences were highly documented and if the information was directly related to the student's course work and portfolio purposes. In addition, the written presentation of the portfolio, for an 'exemplary' rating, would include expected institutional format requirements and be written clearly with proper grammar, punctuation, and spellings.

Those individuals who are already in teaching positions would plan and develop a portfolio for the purpose of gaining tenure, demonstrating teaching styles, or providing evidence that professional educational goals had been achieved. It has been shown that high quality teachers seek opportunities to improve.

THE CONTENTS OF A TEACHING PORTFOLIO

The *teaching portfolio* commonly includes an item that details the teacher's education/teaching philosophy. A quality portfolio would include specific examples of how this philosophy has influenced the teachers' practice. The teaching specialties should be detailed with documents that show a specific lesson plan and the implementation of the teacher's philosophy. For example, how might the contention that the teacher gave specific attention to a student's learning style be documented?

Examples of the teacher's growth and development that has taken place over time through quality experiences are set forth in the teacher portfolio as well. The teacher's success is reflected in examples of 'recognized' standardized tests and learning feedback received from mentors, supervisors, and instructors in higher education. The results of observations of the teacher's performance as well as positive feedback from parents and others serve to document the teacher's achievements.

Philosophy is concerned primarily with pursuits as to what is real, what is true, and what is good. A question commonly posed to a teacher or administrator candidate for a position in the school district is, "What is your philosophy of teaching or of administration?" The same interest is posed in a student portfolio. Cliches, such as 'I just love kids' or 'Teaching is my Life' are not acceptable. Such characteristics should be demonstrated with evidence in the teacher's portfolio.

A school administrator might be asked about their standing on teachers' performance as a factor in determining their compensation. For example, "What is your philosophy on compensation for teachers based on teaching performance?" Attempting to 'make up' one's philosophy on the spot is unacceptable. The point is this: What do you really believe about student learning or student-teacher relationships? Has this question been addressed in the final portfolio?

It is common to read or hear the statement that classroom teaching must be in the best interests and needs of the student. The statement seems to be accepted by teachers, but what percentage of the teachers have this 'piece' of philosophy in their teaching practices? A quality teaching portfolio can loom important in the teacher's plan for growth and development. Specifically, such a portfolio can direct the teacher's attention to areas of strength that should be continued in the instruction plan and also the weaknesses that must be attended. In any case, such information is not restricted to the 'opinion' of one school principal or supervisor, rather the information in a quality portfolio is a reflection of many individuals and sources.

Chism (1998) has pointed out that a teaching philosophical statement should serve to answer several key questions:

- How do students learn?
- How do teachers facilitate that learning?
- What goals do I have for my students?
- Why do I teach the way I do?
- What do I do to implement these ideas about teaching and learning in the classroom?
- Are these strategies working?
- How do I know they are working?
- What are my future goals for growth as a teacher?

Goodyear and Allchin (1998) also made several suggestions for the components which should be included in a teaching portfolio. Their focus, however, is on the faculty personnel in higher education. First, such a portfolio should underscore the three primary 'missions' of teaching, research, and public service. These three purposes not only loom important in promoting the purposes of the university but also loom important for supporting the individual faculty member's success for moving up in the ranks within the university.

How the teacher distributes his or her philosophy into the instructional lessons for the learning of the students is important component of the teaching portfolio. Why do I teach the way I do? That is, just how is 'my' teaching philosophy evidenced in the way I teach and communicate with students.

The importance of 'purpose' in a teacher's portfolio is supported by the examples that support the teacher's actual instructional resources. The specific subjects taught accompanied by grade levels and class sizes must be included in the documentation of the teaching experience. A copy of a lesson plan along with course outlines that detail as what is being taught is of importance.

Important questions to be posed and answered include: What student assessments are employed? What instructional methods/resources are utilized? To what extent are students actively involved in the learning activities? What attention has been given to the learning styles of the students in your classes? How do you assess and evaluate the success of your teaching? The answers to such questions serve the important purpose of documenting the characteristics of one's teaching. However, rather than just naming what activities are employed in teaching, evidence of what specifically was done to achieve the purposes should be demonstrated.

Just how the faculty member keeps abreast of his or her professional field and how this knowledge is shared with students is an essential component of teaching portfolio. Teachers in institutions of higher education are commonly criticized for their small workload. After all, a professor might teach only two or three classes each week. Little do the critics know about the time and effort that go into research and service activities of teachers in higher education.

PROFESSIONAL GROWTH AND DEVELOPMENT

Great teachers are among the very first individuals to seek and implement opportunities for professional growth. As underscored in chapter 1, when professional growth opportunities are not readily available for quality faculty personnel, they have been shown to move elsewhere. This truth is demonstrated at all levels of education, K–12 and in higher education programs. Similar to any other activity to improve one's performance, the development of an improvement plan is recommended. Does my personal portfolio and/or other informational feedback give me a focus for developing an improvement program?

Teaching portfolios need to underscore how the teacher works to improve his or her instruction. Are students learning? What teaching strategies provide evidence that the instruction is or is not effective? The ability to observe other teachers in their classrooms, participating in professional teacher conferences, upgrading lesson plans, piloting new instructional strategies, checking latest textbooks on the market, and assessing the individual academic improvement of students in the classroom are among the many ways that instructional improvement can be realized.

Some documentation recommendations may be somewhat surprising even to those who do teach. For example, various recommendations for documentation include not only courses taught and instructional methods utilized, but recommend that enrollment figures, syllabi, lesson plans, evaluation procedures, reading lists, homework requirements, tests that are implemented, instructional materials utilized, technology used in teaching, teacher load information, class sizes, and related extracurricular assignments be included in the teaching portfolio. Norton has recommended that the secondary and elementary teacher load formulas be used to calculate teacher load data that can be included in the teacher's teaching portfolio (Douglass, 1950; Norton and Bria, 1992).

Student ratings and notes/comments from parents could be helpful in giving feedback relative to the effectiveness of the teacher. However, by others frequently are related to the teacher's affective characteristics such as friendliness, caring, and fairness. Teaching effectiveness is best demonstrated by student academic improvement including scores on standardized tests, improvements by students in written assignments, scores on pre- and post-quizzes, oral class participation, and other creative work that a student has completed.

THE LIGHTBULB BLEW OUT

Merlin George was a new administrative hire in a large school district in Kansas. He was named the assistant superintendent for curriculum which was the first administration office of this kind in the district. Dr. George was highly qualified for the position. He had previous experience as a teacher and curriculum coordinator in a large school district in Nebraska.

During the reporting week for teacher at the beginning of the school year, Dr. George scheduled a meeting with the teaching faculty for the purposes of 'setting forth' his relationship with faculty personnel and briefly expressing his philosophy relative the school district's curricular program and the ways in which the members could work together to accomplish the best learning environment for students.

The entire teaching faculty and administrative personnel were in attendance. Following George's brief introduction, one member of the teaching faculty spoke out, "Why not just leave us the hell alone, we're professionals!" George was new to the district and the entire faculty and administration were present as well as the school superintendent. Take a moment and place yourself in the 'role' of Merlin George. What might you do at this time? Just smile and move on? Ask the teacher to explain himself? Or do something else?

George moved on to tell briefly about his experiences with professional teachers and their personal interest and need to improve. He noted that improvement was vested in the minds and hands of those professionals in the audience today. He noted that parents and students were counting on the school professionals to implement a learning environment within the school community. He emphasized that 'all of us' thinking and working together can achieve the purposes for which we were hired and that is to make certain that students were given the very best opportunity to meet their own personal interests and needs.

In brief, George received a standing ovation. Curricular achievements within the school district over time were revolutionary.

It is important to keep in mind that a teacher's philosophy statement certainly will change over time. New growth and insights into one's teaching experiences and growth development serve to change the teacher's thinking about such matters as to how students learn, how best to determine a student's learning style, and how my teaching style is being received by the students in my classes. Give thought to how the teacher might demonstrate this characteristic. That is, what evidence would serve to show that the teacher was knowledgeable about learning styles and their importance?

In any case, a quality portfolio can serve the teacher and the school program in a variety of positive ways. For example, the portfolio can serve the teacher well in professional activities such as seeking teaching positions, applying for responsible positions within the school system, seeking openings in school districts for administrative personnel, informing parents and other in the school community about his or her teaching effectiveness, and last but not least, a positive sense of personal satisfaction for the success that has been achieved over a specific time period.

A CLOSER LOOK AT STUDENT LEARNING STYLES: A MUST FOR EFFECTIVE TEACHING

The contention that effective teaching focuses on the individual student's interests and needs has been mentioned previously in the chapter. It is well known that many authorities have promoted the importance knowing each *student's best learning style*. As is true with most every 'theory' in education, there are supporters and non-supporters of this contention. Johns (2020) is one of the strong supporters of knowing the differences in the learning styles of students. As stated by Johns (2020, August 20), "Recognizing these differences affords children best education possible" (p. 1).

Four learning styles are commonly mentioned by supporters of this concept: spatial and visual, tactile and kinetic, auditory, and logical. Adapting instruction content and methods to a student's success level and learning style has been demonstrated in numerous studies to improve student performance. In fact, adjusting learning to students' strengths and interests is a strong characteristic of effective teachers (Norton, 2015).

As previously noted, four types of learning styles have been recognized. *Visual learners* prefer seeing and observing things; seeing diagrams, pictures, and using other visual strategies for presenting learning that best suits the visual learner. The *auditory learner* excels when the teacher is presenting a lesson or using other auditory methods for instructional purposes. *Kinesthetic learners* prefer doing things and getting involved in the learning activity. Actively getting involved in the learning activity serves this learner best. Some learners learn best by using the written word. Reading the lesson or writing a research report serves this learner as does using the written word in a story or searching the internet for information.

Fostering the best learning by knowing and using a student's best learning style hold many implications for developing a student portfolio. Helping a student find and use the information needed in his or her portfolio is enhanced by staging the environment to facilitate the learning style of the student. It is apparent that the strategies for gathering/learning information are somewhat different for students with different learning styles. The reading/writing learners prefer to learn through written materials. A kinesthetic learner would much more prefer to be involved actively in the learning process. A hands-on activity is preferred. Teachers who are knowledgeable of the concept of learning styles are in a better position to help plan and supervise a student's portfolio completion.

KEY CHAPTER IDEAS AND RECOMMENDATIONS

- In the professional field of education, portfolios have been used for a variety of purposes including course learning, internship logs, field project journals, activity mappings, and as a means to demonstrate personal growth and development.
- Reports indicate that student portfolios are being used by some 90% of the administrator preparation programs surveyed.
- Portfolios have been used successfully in administrator licensing programs within the states.
- A degree licensing program commonly uses portfolios that are presented near the close of the program. Best work is presented with artifacts that show evidence of learning and the applications of the learning results.
- Documentation is a key word in the presentation of administrator portfolios. Have licensing requirements been met? What documents and artifacts serve to show such results?
- A scoring rubric is the common method used for grading a portfolio. Ratings of exemplary, proficient, emerging, and unacceptable are examples of assessment/evaluation results.
- Philosophy is one of the most common entries on portfolios related to human performance. "What is your philosophy relative to student retention in grade?" This is an example of a question often posed in a job interview related to education.
- The key contents for an education portfolio commonly are viewed as teaching, research, and public service.
- Professional growth and development are the supporting foundations for a quality portfolio in education. Great teachers and administrators seek opportunities to improve. A quality portfolio will reveal this contention.
- Student learning styles have been discussed throughout this book. Nevertheless, the importance of student learning styles comes to the fore whenever an individual contemplates the initiation of a professional portfolio.

REFERENCES

Bombeck, W. (1974). Groups vs. individual decision-making. An unpublished doctoral Dissertation. Arizona State University. Department of Educational Administration and Policy Studies. Tempe, Arizona.

Chism, N. V. N. (1998). Developing a philosophy of teaching statement. *Essays on Teaching Excellence*, 9(3), 1–2. Professional and Organizational Development Network in Higher Education.

Douglass, H. R. (1950). *The 1950 Revision of the Douglass High School Teaching Load Formula. NASSP Bulletin*, 35, 13–24.

Goodyear, G. E. and Allchin, D. (1998). Statement of Teaching Philosophy. *To Improve the Academy 17, 103-22.* Stillwater, OK: New Forums Press.

Johns, S. (2020, August 20). *Four Learning Styles.* From the web https://www.the-classroom.com/four-learning-styles-5179201.html

Norton, M. S. (2004). Student learning portfolios: How they are being implemented in educational administration preparation programs. *Planning and Changing*, 35(3 & 4), 223–33.

Norton, M. S. (2015). *Teachers with the Magic: Great Teachers Change Student's Lives.* Rowman and Littlefield, Lanham, MD.

Norton, M. S., and Bria, R. (1992). Toward an equitable measure of elementary school teacher load. *Record in Educational Administration and Supervision*, 13(1), 62–66.

Chapter 4

Important Portfolios with Various Purposes

Primary chapter goal: This chapter continues the exploration of various kinds of portfolios and their specific purposes. Information relative to how schools and other professions are using portfolios in their operations is presented with operational examples.

The teaching portfolio is used primarily for summative purposes. That is, the portfolio is used primarily for getting a teaching position, getting credit for course work, initiating planning, or other promotion purposes. On the other hand, a formative portfolio centers on purposes related to personal improvement toward gaining the credentials for a teaching degree.

It is important to keep in mind that a portfolio is not a complete record of all of the work experiences that the individual has attended. Rather, it is a selection of the actual work/experiences that reveal the nature of the individual's life work and the evidence of their positive influence on one's cognitive knowledge/skills and the affective characteristics that guide one's behavior.

Documents such as examples of student work and improved testing results can be used in the portfolio to demonstrate student growth over time. Professional development is documented in several ways including the receipt of teaching awards and special recognition by a supervisor or letters received from parents, former students, and various professional organizations. Participation in and contributions to the work of the individual's professional organizations commonly demonstrate efforts to keep up to date in one's career field.

PORTFOLIOS FOR EDUCATIONAL ADMINISTRATOR PROGRAM ADMISSION, PROGRAMS OF STUDY, AND FIELD EXPERIENCES

Each state has its specific requirements for completing a university or college degree and for licensing a school principal or other primary school administrators. The student's portfolio, in turn, must meet the standards of the university department in which the degree program is offered. The requirements for the initiation and completion of an administrator portfolio are of paramount importance. If the specific initiation and completion requirements for the portfolio are not followed, the portfolio is not likely to be approved.

One of the most popular portfolios is one that centers on individuals that aspire to the leadership role of school principal. It is of interest to note that a large percentage of master's degrees awarded to teachers is for specialization in educational administration and not for elementary or secondary school education. The point here is that a portfolio for an individual, who is aspiring to an administrative position, can serve to emphasize the strengths and skills sought by school boards and other school leaders for leadership positions.

LEADERS' PROGRAM PORTFOLIOS

A leadership program plan initiates the designing of the graduate student's program of studies and the beginning of the student's leadership/portfolio plan for initiating and completing the degree and licensing program. It is at this point that the student begins to assume a greater responsibility for entering and completing a highly successful degree/licensing program. A major part of this responsibility is vested in the initiation of an administrator portfolio.

A survey was sent to several national programs that prepared educational administrators. The survey letter simply asked the chair or director of the university's administration program to answer ten questions that centered on the current use of portfolios in their preparation programs. It was interesting to note that each of the 25 participating chairs indicated that portfolios were indeed being utilized in their department's administrator programs. The specific purposes and the percent of response are shown in table 4.1.

Table 4.1 Portfolio Uses in Preparation Programs

Specific Purposes	% Response
a. Requirement for an internship	73.7
b. Part of course requirements	52.6
c. In lieu of comprehensive exam	47.4
d. Evaluate administrative skills at the beginning, middle, and end of program	42.1
e. Fieldwork or other practicum	36.8
f. Entry year assessment requirement	10.6
g. Decide continuation in program	10.6
h. Part of the state's requirements	10.6
i. Explore research/dissertation topic	5.3
j. Admission requirement	5.3

It is evident that the leading three uses of portfolios centered on skill assessment as related to specific course and/or field requirements. Portfolio uses for purposes of student admission, program continuation, achievement of state requirements, or research topic exploration were much less significant. Only 10.6% of the institutions used student portfolios to assess entry year performance, to decide continuation in the program or to assess the achievement of certain state standards.

It is of interest to note, however, that those institutions using portfolios almost always tied them to one or more sets of broad standards commonly set by NCATE (National Council for the Accreditation of Teacher Education) standards for admission and slightly less than one-third focused on ISLLC (Interstate Standards Leadership Licensure Consortium) standards. Such standards nationally historically seem to come and go. As is commonly the case, institutional practices tend to tie closely to standards such as those promoted by the aforementioned institutes. Yet, like old soldiers, they most often just fade away.

Table 4.2 sets forth study findings related to the utilization of student learning portfolios in the 90 university programs.

It is noted that the foregoing survey was taken prior to the entry of Covid-19 upon the education scene in 2020. Whether or not the use of student portfolios has been extended within the last few months, when the virus pandemic was affecting almost every university program in the nation, was not known at the time of the writing of this book. Nevertheless, with the closing of most

Table 4.2 Programs Using Student Learning Portfolios in Preparation Programs in Educational Administration

Study sample	90
Respondents	63 (70%)
Respondents using portfolios	57 (90%)
Degree/Certification Programs	*Percent of Subgroup Using Portfolios (%)*
Master's degree	89.5
Educational Specialist (EdS)	36.8
EdD degree	26.3
PhD degree	31.6
Certification/Licensing	47.4

university programs and the movement toward digital learning, it could be assumed that portfolios have increased in administrative programs nationally.

In many states, K–12 schools have closed. Some have reopened and then closed once again. It has been shown that some teachers and administrators have 'refused' to return to the opening of schools in their school districts due to the virus pandemic. Additionally, the strategy of 'training' school administrators, prior to the advent of Covid-19, was to have the student experience administration in a school district's school. Just what happens to this arrangement when the school closes is not clear. The principal, who had been serving as the student's 'mentor,' is likely to have been furloughed and unavailable at the school. The student's portfolio plan most certainly is in jeopardy.

We underscore the program interruptions during the virus pandemic by quoting the documentation requirements for field-based internship work within one university. In almost every university, such educational requirements/provisions become impossible and some other innovative strategies must be planned and implemented unless students' plans are set aside and impossible to implement.

The documentation of field-based internship work at one institution of higher education is required as follows. Keep in mind that the following requirements were in force before the Covid-19 pandemic came on the national scene.

> The licensing program requires 7 semester credits of field work for all students. Some of the work is done each semester and related to the domain of study each semester being focused on at that time. A summer intensive internship of 3 semester credits is competed near or tat the end of the licensing program.

Table 4.3 Uses of Student Portfolios Relative to Various Degree and Certification Programs

Specific Portfolio Uses	Percent Response (%)				
	MEd	EdS	EdD	PhD	Cert.
Program admission	5.3				
Comprehensive exam	47.4	15.8	5.3		10.6
Course requirement	63.2	26.3	10.6	15.8	42.4
Internship requirement	69.4	21.1	10.6	15.8	42.1
Fieldwork/Practicum	47.4	21.1	5.3	5.3	42.1
Independent study					5.3
First Year Assessment	5.3				5.3
End provisional status	5.3				5.3
Final exams in courses	10.6	5.3			10.6

Documentation of work done must be provided for all internship credits. All students should complete 45 contact hours of internships for each semester including the summer semester that related to a specific domain, and all students should complete an intensive internship of not less than 135 contact hours, usually during the summer. Total contact hour requirements for the internship total 315 hours.

Just who would supervise such an extensive field-based program during an pandemic is not clear. Schools are closed, university programs are largely online, and administrative supervisors are on furlough. Few students in administration programs are able to spend full time on field work and internships during the normal school months. That is why some students in administrative programs serve in the positions of teacher and as an administrative assistant in the same school. The problem centers on the fact that many teachers have refused to return to work during the pandemic and so the teachers who do return to school have full teaching loads.

There are several specific implications of student learning portfolios as related to the work climate, responsibilities, and relationships when student portfolios are implemented (Norton 2004). For example, the initiation of student portfolios into practice will require the student to take responsibility for structure and organization of process on a self-directed basis. In addition, student portfolio implementation requires the maintenance of a meaningful focus on relevant learning processes and structure. These changes mean that faculty will be working differently with students. Student involvement in the learning plan and its accomplishment 'changes hand'; the student indeed becomes engaged in his or her own learning activities.

In addition, changes to the utilization are 'revolutionary' for most students and a large percentage of the teaching staff. New and different standards for learning come into play.

Changes in the assessment and evaluation processes come to the fore. Student self-assessment looms increasingly important. In addition, more than one teacher most commonly joins the activities of student grading. Grades as such tend to disappear; rubrics take over the job of 'grading the work' of the student. In short, relationships between students and faculty are increasingly changed. Self-evaluation on the part of the student looms important, but peer and faculty members are increasingly more involved in the student's learning process planning and ultimate evaluation.

THE LEARNING BENEFITS OF STUDENT PORTFOLIOS AS STATED BY FACULTY PERSONNEL

Commonly, the initiation of any new innovation in education finds both support and criticism from the population at hand. Yes, when faculty personnel were questioned regarding the learning benefits of using student portfolio methods, not a single member stated that portfolio methods were not beneficial. Table 4.4 sets forth the responses of faculty personnel as related to their views of student portfolio methods.

In view of the earlier movements toward *competency skill development* and the achievement of administrative leadership standards, it is interesting to note that the study results indicate that student portfolios have considerable potential for adding to the development of administrative skills such as judgment, organizational ability, written and oral communication, problem analysis, collaboration, and others. As one study participant stated, "Portfolios place the student in the very center of the learning process. Learning is more integrated and meaningful."

AN INTERESTING SIDE NOTE: PORTFOLIOS COMPLETED ONLINE

We found it of interest to learn that a person can create their own portfolio online. Portfoliopen, a company located in Amsterdam, NY, advertises the

Table 4.4 Learning Benefits for Students Using Portfolio Methods: Faculty Opinions

Benefits	Percent Responding
Alternative to traditional program practices	
Highly beneficial	38.9
Considerably beneficial	27.8
Moderately beneficial	33.3
Not beneficial	0.0
Allows for individualization	
Highly beneficial	52.9
Considerable beneficial	41.2
Moderately beneficial	0.0
Not beneficial	5.9
Serves as a valuable assessment tool	
Highly beneficial	50.0
Considerably beneficial	33.3
Moderately beneficial	16.7
Not beneficial	0.0
Promotes reflection, transformational leadership, and synthesis of meaning	
Highly beneficial	76.5
Considerably beneficial	19.6
Moderately beneficial	5.9
Not beneficial	0.0
Adds to administrative skills (written, oral, judgment, etc.)	
Highly beneficial	43.8
Considerably beneficial	37.5
Moderately beneficial	18.7
Not beneficial	0.0

creation of online portfolios. In fact, the company offers a free plan, a basic plan, and a pro plan. Each plan has its own contingencies, of course, in regard to mega bites and costs although the free plan is indeed free. It provides for the uploading of ten artworks, 10 MG of disk space. This portfolio, of course, is to introduce you to the company's portfolio plans and motivate you to take up their more sophisticated/costly plans. Although we are not endorsing the company or the product that the company has available, we do want to note the attention that the portfolio business has entered the market.

That is, one tries the free portfolio, then can choose the basic plan, and ultimately gets everything with the pro plan. We call attention to this side note in an attempt to underscore the advancing interest in portfolios, not only in education but in many other professions such as business. Portfoliopen sets forth its *advertisement* in the brief message that follows:

> Portfoliopen is an easy tool to show off your work. It's a worry-free hosted solution, so you don't have to install anything, no setup required, you don't have to worry about hosting, programming, search engine optimization, and other weird things like that—we've taken care of it for you. We're stable, secure, and reliable. We give you a professional looking website so you can focus on your best. However, we don't want to limit your creativity, it's very easy to personalize the overall look of your online portfolio, translate into your language use your own domain. Well, what are you waiting for?

A SUPPLEMENTAL DISCUSSION OF TEACHING PORTFOLIOS: SIMILARITIES OF K–12 AND HIGHER EDUCATION PORTFOLIO PRODUCTS

Student portfolios have been given the most attention thus far and teaching portfolios have been discussed previously in relation to content and assessments. Nevertheless, a primary benefit of the teacher's portfolio is vested in the answer to the primary purposes it serves. A teaching portfolio is, first and foremost, a documentation of one's life as a member of the education profession. The teaching portfolio serves as a positive motivational record of the many ways in which the individual teacher has contributed to the professional business of education. Such a record should set forth the best work of the teacher that serves as a reminder of just how important the person's work has been to students and the welfare of the nation as a whole.

How might a teaching portfolio serve the implementor of such a document? Job applications, tenure documentation, self-improvement programs, self-development evidence, peer communication, and service records all are ways in which a quality teaching portfolio serves the individual. Most recommendations for planning and completing a teaching portfolio recommend that you document information relative to:

Teaching responsibilities and curricular experiences:

1. Your personal philosophy about the importance of teaching, one's thoughts about student and teacher relationships, and the teacher's philosophy relative to relationships, grading, discipline policy/procedures, learning goals/objectives, and teaching strategies.

2. Your teaching specialties including subjects taught and grade level experience.
3. Sample lesson plan(s) that demonstrate the subjects taught, teaching methods, student learning assessments, and student growth.
4. Homework expectations including the time factors and their weight in determining a student's grade.
5. Student involvement strategies.
6. Teacher and parent relations. Communication procedures.
7. Course content.
8. Technology measures for student use.

My record on teaching performance:

1. Documentation of my ability to teach. Records of teacher evaluations and assessments.
2. Service and experience record as a classroom teacher.
3. Examples of parent, student, and peer notes and letters regarding their expressions of 'thanks and appreciation' regarding their experiences and positive results of receiving your instruction and guidance.
4. Include document and best work samples relative to your teaching and its effects on student learning. Include student growth as revealed on standardized tests and other student work results.
5. Professional growth and development activities such as the attendance in education workshops, curriculum committees, professional conferences, and related research activities that focus on your areas of teaching. Include presentations at professional conferences, articles published in referred journals, updated subject area lesson plans, and 'before and after' work papers of students in your subject matter courses.

   In addition, include any special colleague services such as mentoring of new teachers and/or updating strategies for colleagues in your area of specialization.
6. Include the details of any special awards/recognitions received for teaching from any recognized individual, department, teacher group, university, or professional organization. Include other special services that you provided in the way of workshops, conference presentations, and mentoring sessions for teacher/administrator department personnel.

Make note of how any of the foregoing accomplishments affected your work performance.

Keep in mind that, although others do recommend the content of your teaching portfolio, you are the one who makes the final decision of what will be included. The teaching portfolio is not something that one keeps 'locked up' in a desk, rather it is meant to be shared with others and used for job applications, shared with other faculty members, and even made available to the public for review and feedback. It is common for the teacher's portfolio to be distributed on the web. Electronic teacher portfolios have become increasingly more popular.

The teaching portfolio does include the teacher's best qualities and professional work. Nevertheless, effective assessments and evaluations will identify areas of needed improvement. What has been done to recognize these 'weakness'? How might the improvements in those areas be demonstrated? What documentation will serve to demonstrate improvement changes that have been made in your classroom teaching?

For example, documentation of the improvement activities engaged in by the teacher, information relative to the improvement of student learning (i.e., student before and after work evidence, before and after student scores on standardized tests, and feedback given to students/parents on the student's learning) should be give due attention. The availability of teaching portfolios on the web by Portfoliopen was discussed previously in the chapter.

PORTFOLIOS UTILIZED IN UNIVERSITY/ COLLEGE PREPARATION PROGRAMS

Portfolios have increased substantially in programs of higher education in educational administration and related educational degree programs. The virus pandemic has been the primary factor of increasing use of program portfolios. It has been noted previously that portfolios in school administration programs have been set forth in requirements related to field experiences, internships, and research projects. In the following section, an example of a portfolio for one graduate program in administration is presented. The example is not viewed as a 'model' that must be implemented by all administration programs, but rather as an example of how a portfolio can be of positive learning experience that takes place during the completion of the master's degree.

PROCEDURES FOR COMPLETION OF THE COURSE—EDA 501
Lafayette University—Department of Educational Administration and Policy Studies
The Purpose

The course, EDA 501, is a course required for certification for the completion of the master's degree. In any case, a portfolio is utilized for all purposes of the course. A one-week orientation is held with all prospective students for the purpose of clarifying portfolio procedural requirements. Although the course instructor will counsel with students in the course online and in person upon request, the student's appointed advisor will work with the instructor during the entire portfolio process. Although the department of educational administration and policy studies, nor the university, does not require a thesis for graduation and licensing, *the completion of the portfolio is required.*

The completion of the portfolio is ongoing during the completion of the master's degree. Therefore, the student must register for the EDA 501 course sometime during the first and no later than the second semester after his or her admission. At the close of the student's completion of the master's degree courses, the student is required to present the completed portfolio to faculty members that include the EDA 501 course members, the student's assigned advisor, and one or two other members of the department's faculty.

PORTFOLIO CLARIFICATIONS

As previously noted, students must enter the program set forth in EDA 501 upon entering the department or very soon thereafter. Since the portfolio program is ongoing during the entire time of the student's degree program, the very first semester of the student's educational experiences begin upon his or her entry to the degree program. In addition, upon admission to the degree program, a faculty member will be assigned as the student's advisor. The advisor and the EDA 501 course teacher will initiate orientation sessions with the student.

Each course taken by the student has implications for inclusion in the student's portfolio. That is to say, each faculty member that teaches a course in which the student is enrolled should be involved in the completion of the student's portfolio. The student must keep in mind that it is his or her responsibility for scheduling informational sessions with the course instructor. Important information given by the instructor can be included in the student's portfolio both for a learning product and a focus on student needs for growth and development.

We underline the importance of the student's initiative in contacting relative persons for feedback as to the student's growth and development. It will not be sufficient to simply wait for the final grade received in a course to learn just how well the student has done. Growth and development during the degree program must be ongoing. Reporting on feedback in the portfolio at appropriate times will enhance the work quality of the portfolio. Once again, feedback for performance in a single course cannot be determined in full by the final grade received. Personal instructor feedback, scores on quizzes/tests, and special experiences that enhanced the student's learning are all important consideration for inclusion in the student's portfolio.

PRESENTATION OF THE STUDENT PORTFOLIO

The student must take note of the time requirements related to the EDA 501 course and the presentation of the 'completed' portfolio toward the end of the master's degree program. As previously noted, a faculty member 'committee' will serve to attend the scheduled meeting of the portfolio presentation by the student. Thus, the presentation date and time have to be determined and approved during the last semester of the student's program. Therefore, the final portfolio product must be in the hands of the appointed faculty members two weeks before the scheduled student presentation. The student must assume the responsibility for having copies of the portfolio in the hands of the course advisor as stated above. The appointed faculty members must be given time to examine and evaluate the student's portfolio. The completed portfolio is to be submitted in multiple copies (a copy for each committee member) to the course advisor who will distribute copies to each faculty committee member.

THE CONTENTS AND MAKEUP OF THE STUDENT PORTFOLIO

As previously noted, an orientation session for all students enrolled in EDA 501 will be held to discuss the important characteristics of the student portfolio and to answer students' questions about the requirements and procedures. The orientation session will be most effective if the student has studied the following information relating to the contents and makeup of the student portfolio. The following information centers on the several content areas that each portfolio should contain.

Content Area A—the student bio that centers on life purposes. The student's primary interests and educational objectives should be summarized. What has the student accomplished to date and what major goals and objectives are in mind for the future?

Content Area B—the student's knowledge and skills related to administrative leadership is the central focus for this area. What has been learned during your program activities that has provided you with a major understanding of organizational development (OD) and effective leadership? Provide examples of your personal leadership. What did you do to resolve a major problem or implement an effective program? In view of the many different types of leadership, how do you view your personal leadership knowledge and skills? Use all of your course experiences and intern experiences to support your opinions.

Content Area C—focus on your personal growth during the master's degree program of experiences. Once again, detail examples of your growth in the area of leadership and effective decision-making. Avoid simply listing your judgments relative to leadership and governance. Rather, give evidence of your possession of such knowledge and skills. What feedback have you received regarding your 'acceptance' as a school leader? What feedback can you give that supports your contentions?

Content Area D—give your attention to the area of OD. First, how has the topic of OD been presented in the several administrative classes that you have experienced? What field experiences were most impressive programmatically? In brief, how has the concept of POSDCoRB (planning, organization, staffing, directing, coordinating, reporting, and budgeting) been incorporated into your administrative philosophy and practice? Provide evidence and specific examples.

Content Area E—document your knowledge and skills in the area of curriculum and instruction. What competencies do you hold in this important area of educational program development. Place emphasis on change and its importance of leadership. Document those areas in which you feel most skilled. What needs to be done, if anything, to improve your competence in this content area?

Content Area F—focus on the administrative area of human resources (personnel). What are your efficiencies in the area of personnel administration? How are these areas defined in what you have done or what you have learned during your preparation time. Give as many examples as you can that relate to your knowledge and skills in this major area of administration. For example, the problem of teacher retention has faced education historically. What leadership might you be able to provide in reversing this problem? How might you work to improve cooperation within the school or implement a mentoring service within the school. Set forth any evidence that serves to support your contentions regarding the foregoing questions.

PRESENTING THE PORTFOLIO

As previously noted, each student will present their portfolio near the end of their degree program. Commonly, the opening presentation by the student will consume not more than 30 minutes. The portfolio introduction is followed by a questioning period by the committee members at hand. The characteristic of 'smoothness' is demonstrated by the fact that the portfolio moves meaningfully from one section to another That is, the contents of the portfolio are not just attached together, but the elements of growth and understanding are revealed in the way one area of the portfolio flows into the next area.

For each area of the portfolio, examples, illustrations, products, and best work samples are set forth to 'witness' what was learned and how the student moved ahead in growth during the experiences in which he or she participated. Best work examples, mentor comments, faculty member feedback, and any special accomplishments/rewards should be recognized as well. For example, in one case, a student participated in a conference of students of journalism. The student received a first-place award for her editorial writing. A copy of the printed reward is appropriate for inclusion in her portfolio.

In summary, the oral presentation of the student portfolio should underscore each major section from A to E. The 'flow' of the contents should have a logical connection from one area to the other. Best work is emphasized and the strategies/examples of learning growth should be recognized and supported.

PORTFOLIO ASSESSMENT AND EVALUATION

When a portfolio is effectively assessed and evaluated, unlike common grades of A, B, C etc., the student understands what and how the grading was derived. Commonly, a predetermined rubric is used to grade the various sections of the portfolio. A, B, and C grading is abandoned and rubric scoring is used to describe the level of quality of the product. The rubrics of *exemplary*, *proficient*, *emerging*, and *unacceptable* are commonly used for 'grading' the major five sections of the student portfolio is so rated. The same rubric is often used to 'grade' the entire portfolio; however, some committees prefer to use the grade of unsatisfactory for unacceptable student work.

Unacceptable final scoring is applied most commonly when the student does not complete the portfolio on scheduled time; receives only emerging or unacceptable scores on one or more areas of the portfolio; and demonstrates that the work in the portfolio is determined not to be that of the student at hand.

Unacceptable student portfolios are handed in various ways. For example, a student with unsatisfactory rubrics most commonly is required to redo and/or improve the unacceptable portions of the portfolio and, with the approval of the faculty advisor, reschedule another portfolio presentation as fits the case. A second unacceptable scoring of a student's portfolio is handled in several ways. Each case is rated on its own merits. Most often, a second student presentation is scheduled and the same faculty members once again 'score' the portfolio results.

Who commonly serves as reviewers for portfolio assessments and evaluations? At the K–6 levels, it is common for the student's main teacher and two other teachers to serve on the assessment committee. At the higher education level, the student's program advisor, portfolio reviews committee, course instructor, oral defense committee members, specific faculty members @ purposes, ad hoc committee @ purposes, school site supervisor, other students, and inter-teachers all serve on such committees from time to time and as fits the case.

PORTFOLIO PROJECTS FOR COURSES IN HIGHER EDUCATION

There is some evidence that the use of portfolios in courses in higher education have increased since the beginning of the virus pandemic that took hold in the early months of 2019. Many universities in the United States had portfolio requirements in place long before the problems of the pandemic closed many education institutions across America. Auburn University, for example, had a portfolio program in place in 2016 that centered four primary characteristics: critical thinking through reflection, visual literacy, technical competency, and effective communication. The following material is based on Auburn's Portfolio Project and is an excellent example of quality work.

Auburn University representatives introduce their Portfolio Project (2016) by commenting on the important purposes of their program. As the Office of University Writing note: Portfolios can take many forms, but for the purpose of assessing the outcome associated with this project, we expect an ePortfolio to tell a coherent story about the student's learning experiences both in and out of classes, synthesize and present those experiences for a general, external, professional audience. ePortfolios of this kind provide evidence of skills and interests through a curated selection of artifacts and craft in the process of professional identity.

In regard to the characteristic of critical thinking, the evidence of artifacts, arrangement, and reflective writing is underscored. The evaluation rubrics of beginner, developing, mature, and professional are used to score/evaluate the student's portfolio. It is beyond the scope of this chapter to detail each of the major characteristics. However, the feedback for rubric citations are especially well stated and the characteristic of *artifacts* is stated below to demonstrate the rubric levels utilized in the portfolio assessment and evaluation.

CRITICAL THINKING THROUGH REFLECTION: ARTIFACTS

1. Beginner: included artifacts show little connection to overarching story or the story itself is missing. Artifacts are not contextualized so their meaning is supplied more by the viewer than the author. There is little variety of skills, experiences, and learning represented and not enough

Table 4.5 Contents of the Student Portfolio

Area A—Scoring for resume, goals and objectives, future considerations
Student Portfolio Give Attention to (circle correct response):

1. Personal Resume	Plus	Minus
2. Professional Goals and Objectives	Plus	Minus
3. Summary of Accomplishments	Plus	Minus
4. Future Objectives	Plus	Minus

Area B—Knowledge of Administration

1. Understanding of OD	Plus	Minus
2. Leadership Knowledge	Plus	Minus
3. Growth/Learning Demonstrated	Plus	Minus
4. General Knowledge of Educational Administration	Plus	Minus

Area C—Evidence of Growth/Learning

1. Personal Growth	Plus	Minus
2. Evidence of School Leadership	Plus	Minus

Area D—Breadth of Administration Knowledge

1. Knowledge of OD Principles	Plus	Minus
2. Knowledge of Depth of Administration	Plus	Minus

Area E—Program Development

1. Knowledge of Curriculum Development	Plus	Minus
2. Identification of Curriculum Skills	Plus	Minus

Overall Scoring for each of the five areas above:

1. Scoring on Area A   Exemplary___ Proficient___ Emerging___ Unacceptable___
2. Scoring for Area B   Exemplary___ Proficient___ Emerging___ Unacceptable___
3. Scoring for Area C   Exemplary___ Proficient___ Emerging___ Unacceptable___
4. Scoring for Area D   Exemplary___ Proficient___ Emerging___ Unacceptable___
5. Scoring for Area E   Exemplary___ Proficient___ Emerging___ Unacceptable___

Committee Member Comments, Explanations, and Recommendations

_____   _____
Name of Committee Member   Date

---

evidence to support the claims being made. Most artifacts are of the same kind or from the same kind of experience (e.g., course papers or images of design work).

2. Developing: some artifacts contribute to the story being told, but limited and individual artifacts have little contextual information to support their inclusion. While the overarching story is not supported by all of

the artifacts, there are some moments where artifacts do substantiate the claims.
3. Mature: most artifacts provide evidence of the story being told and most support claims being made. Artifacts are contextualized so that the reason for their inclusion is almost always clear. The artifacts provided demonstrate a variety of skills, experiences, and learning across a range of courses or cocurricular experiences.
4. Professional: artifacts provide strong evidence of the story being told and claims being made. Artifacts are well contextualized so that their presence in support of a message is clear throughout. The artifacts provided demonstrate a variety of skills, experiences, and learning and draw from a wide range of experiences both in and out of formal courses.

We note, once again, that the four rubric assessments are provided for the assessment and evaluation and along with the major two other characteristics of visual literacy and technical competency. The rubrics for portfolio-based assessment range from 0 to 3 (0: does not meet expectations; 1: partially meets expectations; 2: meets expectations; and 3: exceeds expectations). It is common for portfolios to be assessed on several basic criteria: sources of learning, demonstration of learning, evidence of learning, mastering knowledge and skills, reflection on learning, and the presentation of the portfolio are such examples.

A CHANGE OF PLACE: THE WIDE UTILIZATION OF BUSINESS PORTFOLIOS

How Are Portfolios Utilized in Many Businesses?

A *business portfolio* (My Accounting Course 2020, August 21) is a set of company's products, services, strategic business units that conform a given company and allow it to pursue its strategic goals. This portfolio can also be defined as the set of available assets that the company possesses to develop its mission and reach its vision. (p. 1–4) Two 'related' portfolios, the business and product portfolios, differ in that the business portfolio focuses on a wider range of elements such as productive, equipment, machinery, and fixed assets. On the other hand, the product portfolio is concerned only with the physical items sold by the company.

A business portfolio places emphasis on its compilation of products and services that the company can offer to the *target market*. All available products and services are included in the compilation, not only the new or latest ones that the company offers. At best, the company's business portfolio can be instrumental in clarifying just how it can become more competitive by implementing new strategies to improve its growth. As author With (2020) points out, management looms important on all three levels of a business portfolio including managers for managing individual products, managing product lines, and top-level management that oversees the company's completed portfolio. Each level of management focuses on the overall goal of making the organization become 'the best that it can be.'

A business portfolio could be developed that is assessed and evaluated by all units of the company revealing what products/businesses have the most potential for increased growth and profitability. A quality business portfolio will serve to help the company take measures to increase the attention of employees for taking advantages of its resources. This important objective is crucial for helping the company reach its business purposes. In addition, an effective business portfolio helps in the planning and analyzing its best products and service practices. The winners are increased and the losers set aside. That is, information relative to financial matters such as market sales and profits, personnel and product costs, and product/service winners and losers all can be determined, assessed, evaluated, and increased or dropped from company's portfolio.

The Steps toward the Development and Implementation of a Business Portfolio

There is no one model for developing and implementing a business portfolio. Nevertheless, there are several recommended steps that have served the administration of administrative practices such as change and administrative improvement. Several recommended steps for initiating and completing a business portfolio are summarized in the following section.

Act 1—Checking the Company's Understanding of Portfolios

What they are, what purposes portfolios might serve, how a company portfolio serves the employees, who does the work, and why must everyone be involved in planning and developing the company's business portfolio. Act 1 commonly assumes a more informal discussion whereby company members become informed as to why such a strategy is needed and how it could serve toward new growth and development for the company.

Depending on the size of the company, the 'informal discussions' might have to be initiated by having smaller groups within the company meet, confer, ask questions, and provide input that helps to foster a better understanding of the portfolio process and the members' involvement in its planning and development.

Act 2—The Focus on the Three Ps of Portfolio Implementation: Purpose, Purpose and Purpose

The Common Components of a Business Portfolio

A brief statement of the company's history commonly is set forth in a brief introduction. Nevertheless, the three Ps of the company constitute the primary introduction of the company's portfolio. Thus, Act 2 in its development serves to answer several key questions. It is necessary to point out, that Act 2 not only is important for the company's potential clientele, but serves as a meaningful 'exercise' for the employees.

What is the company's history? Who opened the company originally and for what primary reasons? Who was being serviced by the company during its early years and are these groups/persons the same now as was the case historically? If the company has been in operation for a longer period of time, what services have been most important for its continuation? Has the company remained competitive over the years and what services have tended to keep the company competitive? What about the company's present purposes? Are these purposes still relevant in today's business operatives? Why or why not?

Act 3—The Contents/Products of the Company

Specifically, what are the products and services that are provided by the business? Discuss/illustrate/show examples of the business' products and services. Photographs and illustrations of what the business can 'do for you' should be given high priority. Do not only describe the products, but use the most ingenious examples that members of the company can derive for illustrating why everyone should have the opportunity to use them advantageously. Before and after photos, remarks from the mouths of continuing customers, and illustrations of how the services will add to the enjoyment of life should be included in the portfolio.

True examples of customer's appreciation with the businesses products and service are necessary and appropriate. False advertising of any kind will surely result in a loss of the company's trust. Include examples of problems faced and how the company took charge in finding a highly acceptable solution to the problem. Bad news is said to travel fast, but good news will win the race overall.

Act 4—View the Portfolio as an Ongoing Goal/Objective of the Company

In education, schools commonly have large policy and regulation manuals that sit on the shelves of a teacher's classroom gathering dust. Although there is no attempt here to compare education policy manuals with teacher portfolios, business portfolios, to be effective, must be ongoing, readily available, assessed/evaluated regularly, and used to foster needed changes/improvements as needed and not just at the close of a school year. Similarly, a business portfolio is only as beneficial as how it is updated, assessed/evaluated, and discussed on a regular business basis.

New services and new products must be documented and disseminated. Additions/changes to the business portfolio always will be ongoing. If not, the stagnation will most likely be revealed in the troublesome changes that appear in the company's sales and operations. Up-to-date and attractive business portfolios tend to carry the message of the fact that things are progressing relative to the goals and objectives that the company set forth at the outset of the portfolio program.

In-service collaboration sessions on the status of the company's business portfolio are essential. Change is ever present in world affairs and in business practices. Corresponding business practices are in this world of change.

Along with the three Ps of portfolio development, there is a formula for the business portfolio. The formula is: $BP = P^2 + S + P \times W\infty$ (business portfolio equals double purpose + service + products multiplied by work to the infinity).

According to With, product portfolio management is one of the most crucial elements of the entire business strategy. That is, product portfolio management is most helpful to the company for helping to attain its major business objectives and for planning the future line of products. In addition, it serves to provide the company essential information relating to profit margins market shares and operational risks. In short, the main role of product portfolio management is to analyze which products are well aligned with the overall strategy and objectives of the business.

With sets forth the primary importance of product portfolios in the business areas of product innovation, tax benefits, projects and businesses strategy, visualization of the entire product line, allocation of resources, data resource, cash flow issues, firm management, and product management. With concludes his excellent discussion of business portfolios by noting that "portfolio management is a must for enterprises and it leads to a strong organization with planned goals and optimum resource allocation" (p. 6).

A FOUR-CHAPTER TRUE/FALSE QUIZ

1. The term *documentation*, as it relates to student portfolio development, centers on how the student used examples and illustrations to demonstrate the evidence that the portfolio requirements had been fulfilled. True____ or False____
2. A *rubric* is the term used for the scoring method which is used to rate the contents of a student or other kind of portfolio. True____ or False____
3. Since a student portfolio is personal in nature, the information in the portfolio should be protected from access by the public in general. True____ or False____
4. Available research has shown clearly that a teacher's educational philosophy is unlikely to change over time. True____ or False____
5. Both scientific and empirical research have underscored the fact that decisions made by a knowledgeable group most often is superior to decisions made by a knowledgeable individual. True____ or False____
6. A teacher's portfolio should avoid including material that might be viewed as being too self-serving such as honors received and service to state and/or national education associations. True____ or False____
7. In one study reported in chapter 2, more than 90.0% of the school administrators did use portfolios for many educational purposes in their preparation programs. True____ or False____

8. School policy and regulation manuals serve much the same purposes as does a school portfolio or an administrative portfolio. True____ or False____
9. A business portfolio focuses on documenting the policies and regulations of the company. True____ or ____False
10. A business portfolio is the collection of products and services provided by the company. True____ or False____
11. Authorities state that there are two main kinds of business portfolios, products and business portfolios. True____ or False____
12. Although teaching portfolios serve many purposes, it is not to be used for such purposes as documenting the teacher's teaching performance. True____ or False____
13. A list of courses taught, extracurricular assignments, and examples of lesson plans are examples of documentation of the teacher's teaching effectiveness. True____ or False____
14. Although what the teacher believes about the education profession is important, the teacher's teaching philosophy is not something that should be included in his or her education portfolio. True____ or False____
15. The formula, $BP = P^2 + S + P \times W\infty$ is a portfolio formula included in chapter 2. The formula was developed by Albert Einstein during his tenure at Princeton University. True____ or False____

ANSWERS TO THE QUIZ

1. The answer to statement #1 is true. The term *documentation* centers on how the contents of the portfolio are accompanied by examples and accompanying context that explains what was done, how it was presented, and what evidence demonstrates how well it served the stated purposes of the activity.
2. The answer to statement #2 is true. Letter grades are seldom found in portfolio assessments. Rather, it is common to find numbers assigned to various content in the portfolio or as an overall rating of the portfolio's quality. For example, the numbers 1 to 3 might be assigned to various sections of the portfolio and/or to the final product. Commonly, a rubric such as 1 (unsatisfactory), 2 (emerging), 3 (proficient), and 4 (exemplary) is used for assessing/evaluating a portfolio.

3. The answer to #3 is false. On the contrary, a primary benefit of a quality teacher portfolio is to have a document that the student/teacher can share with colleagues and others. Although a student portfolio includes personal information about one's life/work experiences, it is not a diary. Yet, the individual's philosophy about life is often revealed in statements of beliefs, values, and personal life experiences.
4. The answer to #4 is false. To the contrary, personal information relative to one's philosophy about education, student learning, and other beliefs is necessarily an important in one's portfolio. What do you think about sex education for students in the elementary grades? Comment on the adage that 'No Student Shall be Left Behind.' A school board might ask you in an interview for a teaching position, "What do you think about compensation being based on the teacher's teaching performance?"
5. The answer to question #5 is false. Although there certainly have been occasions when an individual came up with a decision that proved to be better than the one made by a group of individuals, studies by Bombeck (1973) and others have researched that question and have shown that group decisions on a matter are better than a decision on the matter by a single entity.
6. The answer to question #6 is false. In fact, a student's portfolio necessary must contain information about his or her achievements and honors received. Information such as the individual's academic standing in his or her high school graduation class, personally authored articles that have been published in refereed journals, important positions held in one's field of education, speeches given at professional conferences, and other such honors loom important in portfolios which are used for position employment, receiving tenure, or being elected to an important position within the school system or the school community.
7. The answer to question #7 is true. Although the study reported in this chapter is somewhat dated, it was cited to demonstrate the fact that the use of portfolios is not new but has been in practice for many years. In addition, because of the disruption of the public schools in America due to the virus pandemic, the implementation of student portfolios might well be re-implemented. That is, student learning during the pandemic might profitably be implemented. We recommend its implementation due to its high potential for increasing student learning.

Important Portfolios with Various Purposes 83

8. The answer to question #8 is false. School board policy and regulation manuals have no direct relationships with student, teacher, or administrator portfolios. School policies set forth what it is that the education programs in the school district are responsible for accomplishing. Administrative regulations answer the question as to how those purposes are to be accomplished. School board policies and regulations set forth the purposes and procedures for all employees within the school district. On the other hand, a student or teacher portfolio is directed to the work of one individual. This is not intended to set aside the fact that a teacher's portfolio necessarily does include evidence relative to how a teacher is fulfilling a requirement of the school board or administrative supervisor.

9. The answer to question #9 is false. A business portfolio is of two kinds, products and services. What are the products of the business and what is the success of each one of them? What are the company's leading products from a marketing point of view? What products are lagging in sales and should any one of them be discontinued. What about the efficacy of the company's services? Change is ongoing. Are the company's services keeping up and even surpassing other competitors? The procedures given to the business portfolio differ significantly from those set forth in a school districts policy and regulation manual.

10. The answer to question #10 is true. As noted in the former question #9, a business portfolio focuses on products and services.

11. The answer to question #11 is true. We purposely have tried to emphasize the content makeup of a business portfolio. Questions 9, 10, and 11 have expressed the major components of a business portfolio. In chapter 3, a more complete example of a business portfolio is presented and discussed.

12. The answer to question #12 is false. The status of the teacher's teaching performance is near the top of the importance ladder. It is certain that the teacher's teaching performance is of first importance in considering the hiring of the individual. Evidence of teacher evaluations, letters of commendation by parents, student comments, and other 'reward' information should definitely be underscored in the teacher's portfolio.

13. The answer to question #13 is true. Although supervisor ratings of classroom teaching performance are evidence of importance, other evidence such as lesson plans, student test improvements, positive notes from

parents and others, and the success of students in follow-up courses in math, science, and others is important as well.

14. The answer to question 14 is false. In an interview session for a teaching position in a school, one of the early questions posed to the interviewee is, "What is your philosophy of education and teaching?" Answers such as "I just love kids" or "I've always wanted to be a teacher" tend to fall short of the mark. Answers related to how the teacher focuses on learning, determines a student's learning interests and needs, and what strategies are implemented to motivate student learning are those expected by the interviewers. How does the teacher determine a student's learning style or find out about a student's personal interests and needs? It could be said that a teacher without a teaching philosophy that guides him or her in meeting goals and objectives is operating in a vacuum.

15. The answer to question #15 is completely false. One thing is certain, the formula has no relationship whatsoever to Einstein. The formula, $BP = P^2 + S + P \times W\infty$, is the author's poor joke that says: business portfolios are services plus products multiplied by work to the power of infinity (it never ends).

YOUR QUIZ SCORE

0 to 4 correct is Unsatisfactory, 5 to 8 correct is Emerging, 9 to 12 correct is Proficient, and 13 to 15 correct is Exemplary.

KEY CHAPTER IDEAS AND RECOMMENDATIONS

- The requirements for the initiation of an administration portfolio are of primary importance. If the specific requirements are not completed, the portfolio is unlikely to be approved.
- The initiation of a portfolio within a company is available to almost everyone. That is, the company will complete the portfolio online using your information and direction. Of course, there is a cost. The more detailed the portfolio, the higher the cost.
- Teaching portfolios can serve many purposes including job applications, tenure documentation, self-improvement programs, and peer collaboration and cooperation.

- A business portfolio is a set of available assets that the company possesses relative to produces and services. Businesses commonly contend that the company develops its portfolio to reach its mission and its visions.
- There is no one model for developing a business portfolio. Commonly, a business portfolio comes off as an advertisement of pluses that the company offers clients by way of its products and services.
- Licensing programs demand strict attention to the state and local requirements that one must meet in order to complete an acceptable product. Failure to do so results in an unacceptable portfolio product.
- The common content of a teaching portfolio includes a philosophy, teaching responsibilities, curricular experiences, sample lesson plan(s), student involvement strategies, homework procedures, and student/parent relation activities.
- Documentation of the ability to teach looms of high interest. The teacher's best work must center on this objective.
- A company portfolio has three key foci: (1) to inform members of purposes and expectations, (2) to underscore the company's primary purposes, and (3) to emphasize its products and services. The topic of purposes centers on the company's goals and objectives.

REFERENCES

Goodyear, G. E. and Allchin, D. (1998). Statement of teaching philosophy. *To Improve the Academy* 17, 103–22. Stillwater, OK: New Forums Press.

My Accounting Course (2020, August 21). *What is a Business Portfolio?* From the web: https://www.myaccountingcourse.com/accounting-dictionary/business-portfolio

With, H. B. T. (2020, July 27). *What is Product Portfolio Management?* From the web: https:// www.marketing91.com/product-portfolio/

About the Author

Dr. M. Scott Norton has served as a secondary school teacher of mathematics, coordinator of curriculum for the Lincoln, Nebraska School District, assistant superintendent for instruction, and superintendent of schools in Salina, Kansas, before joining the University of Nebraska as professor and vice chair of the Department of Educational Administration and Supervision. Later he served as professor and chair of the Department of Educational Administration and Policy Studies at Arizona State University, where he is currently professor emeritus.

His primary research and instruction areas include educational leadership, human resources administration, teaching methods, governance policy, the assistant school principalship, competency-based administration, the school principalship, research methods, theory, organizational development, organizational change, organizational climate, and educational program improvement. He has published widely in national journals in the areas of teaching/instructional methods, organizational climate, gifted student programs, great teachers, student retention, organizational change, and others. He has published widely on a variety of educational topics for Rowman and Littlefield Publishers.

Dr. Norton has received several state and national awards honoring his services and contributions to the field of education and educational administration including awards from the American Association of School Administrators, the University Council for Educational Administration, the Arizona School Administrators Association, the Nebraska School Administrators

Association, the Arizona Educational Research Association, Arizona State College of Education Dean's Award for Distinguished Service to the Field, and the Arizona Information Service, and the award for service as President of the College of Education Faculty Association. He presently is serving as a member of the Arizona State University Emeritus College.

Dr. Norton's state and national leadership positions have included service as executive director of the Nebraska Association of School Administrators, member of the Board of Directors for the Nebraska Congress of Parents and Teachers, president of the Nebraska Council of Teachers of Mathematics, president of the Arizona School Administrators Higher Education Division, and member of the Arizona School Administrators Board of Directors, staff associate for the University Council for Educational Administration, treasurer of the University Council for School Administration, state representative for the Nebraska Association of Secondary School Principals, member of the Board of Editors for the American Association of School Public Relations, and member of the governance council for the Arizona State University Emeritus College.

www.ingramcontent.com/pod-product-compliance
Lightning Source LLC
Chambersburg PA
CBHW032031230426
43671CB00005B/272